FLYIN' CHUNKS AND OTHER THINGS TO DUCK

FLYIN' CHUNKS
AND OTHER THINGS
TO DUCK

Memoirs of a life spent doodling for dollars

Dorse A. Lanpher

Foreword by Don Bluth

iUniverse, Inc.
New York   Bloomington

Flyin' Chunks and Other Things to Duck
Memoirs of a Life Spent Doodling for Dollars

iUniverse books may be ordered through booksellers or by contacting:

iUniverse
1663 Liberty Drive
Bloomington, IN 47403
www.iuniverse.com
1-800-Authors (1-800-288-4677)

Because of the dynamic nature of the Internet, any Web addresses or links contained in this book may have changed since publication and may no longer be valid. The views expressed in this work are solely those of the author and do not necessarily reflect the views of the publisher, and the publisher hereby disclaims any responsibility for them.

ISBN: 978-1-4502-6099-2 (sc)
ISBN: 978-1-4502-6100-5 (hb)
ISBN: 978-1-4502-6101-2 (ebook)

Library of Congress Control Number: 2010914983

Printed in the United States of America

iUniverse rev. date: 10/13/2010

For my daughter Lisa
and
grand daughter Holly Conrad

A *note on doodling*

In my subtitle I use the term, doodling for dollars. I don't use the word doodling as a description of my work ethic, but rather to illustrate the fun surprises that the doodling attitude can sometimes bring to one's creative surface, as it did in my life as an artist.

Table of Contents

Foreword by Don Bluth

It is an honor to provide some insight to the author, Dorse A. Lanpher, a man I've had the pleasure of working with for more than a decade. I've known Dorse since our Disney years during the 1970s. He is a man of vivid imagination; one who has always pushed the envelope to find the unusual, the different, and the most exciting visual beauty to put on the movie screen. I've always marveled at his creativity to make the environment for the animated character believable and beautiful.

He is also a courageous man; a pioneer in his field. He left the security of Walt Disney Productions in 1979 to join Gary Goldman, John Pomeroy, myself, and a group of thirteen "renegade" artists who also left Disney Studio to work on an independent production entitled, *The Secret of NIMH*. The desire of our group was to resurrect some of the beautiful production values that seemed to be getting lost due to studio budget constraints. Dorse's personal efforts proved that special effects are an essential part of storytelling. Water, dust, rain, sparkles, smoke, fire etc, are key effects elements in establishing a believable environment in which the characters will act. The challenge of an animator is to get the audience to identify with the characters on screen; the more believable the characters and especially the environment, the better. Dorse is brilliant at creating the latter.

His extraordinary body of work and influence has contributed greatly to taking feature animation out of the 1970s doldrums and into what we now call the 2nd Golden Age of animation. Dorse's name is on the screen credits of many of the most successful animated features of the last two decades.

As a philosopher, it was noted that he was a man of startling common sense. Upon one occasion, he shared with me one of these astounding nuggets of wisdom with the following quote: "The world is bananas, just stay out of its way, and make sure your life isn't." His sense of humor always got me through the tough times. Thank you, Dorse.

Don Bluth

Preface

A friend of mine once said, "Every one has a story to tell." My friend's comment and my sense of wonder set me on this path of writing my history for I wondered about my childhood and my experiences with my parents. Working as an artist for forty-eight years, mostly in the business of animated films, I decided to share my story, writing it for the pleasure of recalling the ups and downs of my past and painting it as well as my words would allow. As I outlined my life, trying to remember those most important driving forces, I realized that it would take several books to tell the story of anyone's life, and the story that I have written is just a slice, a cross-section of my experiences.

Look around you and it will be difficult for you to find an object that isn't part of the natural environment which hasn't been touched by an artist. Your furniture, your dishes, your movies, your automobile, your toothpaste tube, all are the shape and color they are because of an artist involved in the process of creating these things for our use. I was privileged to become an artist, for the work was mostly fun. To make one's life an effort to follow ones passion is never free from struggle but most always a life filled with play. To be rewarded for that play in such a way as to prosper in your culture is a life fulfilled.

Acknowledgments

Thanks to all of those friends, artists, and managers that I've worked with who continually inspired me to better myself.

And thank you, Renae Haines, for your editorial prowess.

Introduction

I've often thought about how little we, as people, friends and family, know of each other. People close to me have survived many of their own personal battles but I have very little knowledge of what solutions they chose to overcome those hardships. It's possible their experience could benefit me in my struggle to be successful at life if I knew more about them, more than just their favorite TV show, movie or celebrity.

The recording of all experience as history is important, not only as a guide to avoiding life's pitfalls, but also as a helpful guide for successfully constructing one's own life. I wanted to share some of my personal experiences that were life changing, and share those professional ups and downs which altered my direction.

My story is everyone's story in that we all must secure a means to provide for our basic ongoing needs while juggling every day's, sometimes serious, life events.

The following story may contain some inaccuracies, my recall was not total, but presented here is the essence of my experiences, as best as I could describe them.

CHAPTER 1
A Bumpy start

The United States of America. Year one begins on the morning of June 10, 1935, in Pontiac, Michigan. Right off there were chunks to duck. Before I was expelled into this world, from what was supposed to be the comfort of the womb, I had some how managed to break my arm and get entangled in the umbilical cord which was wrapped around my neck, cutting off my air supply.

"Oh yes," Mother told me years later, "you were born dead with a broken arm and the doctor had to give you mouth to mouth resuscitation to save you." She seemed to put it so bluntly. I suspect the truth was that I just wasn't breathing, not dead, but Mother liked to dramatize and do it in a way that would set a person back. But my mother always spoke her mind. Both my younger brother, Darrell, and older brother, Don, were apparently ejected into the world without problems; at least I didn't hear of any.

Having lived through that early trauma, I've puttered through life, one day at a time, attempting to understand how it all works. I would have thought by now that I'd have figured it all out so that I could just kick back and enjoy what's left of it. Not so. I used to have a fantasy. A big house with a circular

Ready for the fight, bring it on!

1

My mom and dad, a young George and Mary, they started it!

driveway filled with the cars of my teenage children's friends. We, the family and all the kids' friends, would be in the backyard playing in the swimming pool, all having a wonderful time. As a reality I doubt if I could have been grown up enough to handle that. It never happened.

I was about nine years old when World War II was winding down. That would have been 1944. My mother had an opportunity to visit California with my brothers and me in tow. My cousin Betty and her husband, Willis Holsworth, wanted to make the trip to California and invited us along. Dad had to stay home to work, he didn't have vacation time. We were still in Pontiac at 108 Poplar Street, a street named for the large poplar trees which lined the street and towered over the houses.

When we got home from the trip my mom talked my dad into moving to California, a trial move. Mother loved the sunshine of California so much she wanted to live there. We rented out our house in Michigan and hit the road pulling a two-wheeled trailer behind a 1939 Pontiac sedan with enough belongings to make a start in California. Driving across the Rocky Mountains in those days was terrifying; don't know how the early pioneers did it in oxen drawn wagons. Part of the perilous, cliff-hanging, highway was being rebuilt and in some places it was a dirt road without barriers to stop your car if it decided to go over the edge. At the last stop, before heading into the mountains, my dad had bought chocolate bars for us as a treat, or maybe to give us courage. As we bravely drove that

L to R my younger brother Darrell, Don and me on the right. Mother dressed us well

scary road I held my candy bar tightly in my hand and nervously squeezed it into a melted mess. We finally arrived at our destination but I don't think my dad found much gold in them thar hills of California. We ended up living in a mostly industrial area in a very tiny cottage. It was one of several small cottages in a row of rental cottages on San Fernando Boulevard, in Glendale. I suspect in the 1930's it might have been a motel, it was built like that. Those little houses are all gone now, replaced by industrial buildings.

3

I celebrated my tenth birthday there. My parents gave me a birthday present which was a real ukulele with a song book by *Ukulele Ike*, a popular singer of the 1930's whose movie name was Cliff Edwards. He did the voice of Jiminy Cricket in Walt Disney's animated feature *Pinocchio*. My parents took my brothers and me to see the movie when I was six years old. It was the first movie I remember seeing, my first brush with the art of Walt Disney. Some people say Cliff Edwards was the originator of scat singing but I'm not sure what Louis Armstrong would say about that. I also couldn't know that many years later I would be standing next to Cliff Edwards, Ukulele Ike, in the men's room at the Walt Disney Studios. I didn't have the courage to interrupt him with my ukulele story. To celebrate my tenth birthday that year my parents took the whole family to the Shrine Auditorium, in Los Angeles, to see *The Clyde Beatty Circus* on stage. I still wonder how we could have afforded that. That is the only childhood birthday I remember, where are the other memories?

At the time we lived there, in that little row of cottages, "San Fernando Road", as we called it, was a main highway. This was long before freeways would divert the traffic around Burbank. I guess in the early days it was just a dirt road. It took traffic to and from Los Angeles as it passed right through downtown Burbank, just to the north east of us. The railroad track was across the road so we had every kind of rolling thunder from the biggest trains, the oldest smoke belching jalopies and the biggest rattling, honking diesel trucks coming to or leaving Los Angeles, roaring through downtown Burbank.

We lived there when President Franklin D. Roosevelt died. I was walking home from school one day and there was a lady watering her front yard and she was crying. Being an inquisitive kid and wanting to help I stopped and ask her what was the matter. She said, wiping tears from her reddened face, "President Roosevelt died." I don't think it affected my parents the same way. I don't remember their reaction so I don't think they were as stressed about it as the woman who was watering her yard. I remember her. Even at ten years old I felt her pain.

I don't think my dad liked living in Californy, as he called it. Maybe work was too tough to find. I don't remember what his work was at the time. I think maybe machine shop work. Maybe he missed the seasons of Michigan. I don't know how he talked my mom into moving back east but he did. We were soon to hit that road with all those other noisy machines to find the highway that headed east. We moved back to our house in Pontiac, Michigan. We only lived there about a year when my parents decided it was time to head back to the left coast again, such gypsies. I did finish grammar school there in Michigan, the sixth grade at Wisner Elementary School. My mother had managed to convince my dad to move back to California but I think by that time he was tired of those awfully cold snow filled winters. They even sold the house in Michigan so I guess they didn't plan on returning. We settled in a trailer park on Chestnut Street in Burbank. My two brothers, Mom, and Dad and I all moved into a twenty five foot house trailer. We had to walk to the communal bathrooms rain or shine. We did keep a pot set out at night, just like the French king in the Palace of Versailles, that way if someone had to pee they didn't have to get dressed for the long walk to the bathroom. In the summer my brothers and I would sleep outside on the patio. I don't remember ever wondering why we didn't just live in a regular house. It was kind of neat.

I was eleven years old that first summer we lived in California when my dad talked me into running my own business. He financed me in a "soda pop" venture. My Dad was working in construction, tile work, at a housing tract in the west San Fernando Valley. It was the beginning of the end to the clean air and clear skies of the rural west valley. Dad convinced me to go to work with him and sell sodas to the workers there. It was very hot and they had very little to drink. I filled a large army surplus container with ice and sodas and went with my dad to the housing tract. I pulled my wagon with its load of icy drinks around the tract and sold sodas to the workers. There wasn't a tree or bit of shade for miles and the summer sun pushed the thermometer over one-hundred degrees. The sodas were selling like crazy and as I pulled my wagon around I would pick up the empty soda bottles. The ones I sold and others that had been left behind. The sodas cost me (actually my dad bought the sodas) ten cents and I would get a nickel for every bottle I returned to the store. I charged fifteen cents a bottle so I made at least one hundred per cent profit on every bottle and I sold every bottle I had. There was one problem. I couldn't haul enough sodas out to the tract to keep me busy all day and I got terribly hot, lonely and bored, so this venture only lasted about two days. Who knows? If I had stuck with it I could maybe own the Pepsi Company today.

I got my first real job at John Markam's Woodshop on Chestnut Street in Burbank. My friends, Ace and Danny, worked there and Mr. Markam needed my help. He paid us fifty cents an hour and we worked two hours after school and eight hours on Saturday. We swept floors. We nailed forms. We rubbed white paste into the wood grain of kidney shaped coffee tables, which came in all colors, awful looking things. It was there, working in that woodshop, I first learned that earning money provided a sense of independence. I loved having the money to buy a shirt just because I liked it, real power. I didn't have to ask Mom or Dad. My boss was Gladis, John's wife, she taught me to say "those things", instead of "them things". Since I was from a family which had a serious shortage of formal education "them things" seemed like the way to call attention to something, like "them things over there". She was relentless in her efforts to correct my poor grammar. "Those things, THOSE, things over there," she would sternly say, scaring me. I feared losing my job because of bad grammar so I worked hard at correcting myself. I'm thankful she was so tough on me.

Television was just becoming popular about this time and the magic of it fascinated my friend Danny and me. We would ride our bikes for miles as we searched the valley, stopping at every TV shop to check out the new TV models. I was twelve years old and rollin' in dough, earning about nine dollars a week. So much money I couldn't spend it all so I saved up enough money to buy my family's first TV. I told my dad that I would put a down payment on a TV if he would buy it. I had saved fifty dollars. After all, how many shirts can a kid buy? We got a black and white, 9 inch Hoffman TV. It had a tiny little yellow-green screen that was round except for the flattened top and bottom. I loved the magic of this box. It delivered the world into our house trailer through that little screen. I would stare at anything on that screen. It was magic. I saw Nat King Cole interviewed when he was just starting out as a piano player with a trio. Television made that possible for me at twelve years old. It really seemed magical.

I started the seventh grade at John Burroughs Junior High School because my parents, being straight arrows, were told by the city that the neighborhood we lived in was in the John Burroughs district. All my friends went to a closer school, John Muir Junior High up in town. I guess their parents were outlaws and didn't concern themselves with the rules. The next year I was allowed to attend John Muir Junior High School, with all my friends. That school was later torn down and eventually replaced by an Ikea store; who knows what will be there in another ten years. I felt much better at John Muir with my friends but I did miss the swimming pool at John Burroughs Junior High. I graduated from the ninth grade at John Muir Junior High and received one of those Bank of America awards for being a student that showed some sort of promise as an artist. I had always enjoyed drawing and had begun to hone that ability years earlier by tracing my older brother Don's drawings of World War Two aircraft. He was a good drawer.

That year my maternal grandmother, living in Michigan, got very sick. About the only thing I remember about her was her washing my ears, her bony finger in my ear, feeling like she was trying to stick it clear through my tiny child head. That was when she lived with us for a while when I was about six years old. She threw my wooden pistol, which my Dad had carved for me, into the furnace. This was my first experience with gun control. She didn't like guns, even those carved out of wood by her son-in-law, my dad. It was around this time that I received a report card from school which was all C's, just average. As I remember I was not happy about that but my mother told me that it was okay. I guess she was just trying to take care of me by protecting me from feeling bad about being average. I do remember wondering why she didn't want me to do better when I wanted me to do better. I needed answers, not tolerance. As the summer of 1949 arrived, my grandma was so sick that my folks thought we should move back to Michigan. There must have been more to that story for moving twenty five hundred miles away from the folks in those freeway free days seems a bit much, that is if you plan on running back east for an illness. Driving a car across the country in those days, without freeways, was a long and gruesome task.

I graduated from John Muir Junior High School, said goodbye to all my friends, quit my job at John Markam's Woodshop, and headed back east to start high school, the tenth grade, in a rural area of Michigan. My uncle Caleb lived in Drayton Plains, Michigan, and fortunately for us he had converted his garage into a small cozy house which we made our home. The little house had a pot bellied stove in the middle of the tiny living room. In the winter, which was miserably cold, my dad would fill that stove with coal and it would glow red hot. That stove was a good friend in the winter after spending hours out in the snow, skiing, and skating.

These were nice years. My cousin Sam, who had always lived in Michigan, was two years older than myself and had skis and sleds and hockey sticks. In the winter we would ski and toboggan. If the wind wasn't blowing when the lake froze we would clear the snow and make a hockey rink. If the wind was blowing when the lake froze it would make the ice so bumpy that the lake would be unusable for ice skating for the whole winter. We would be very disappointed. In the summer we would hike in the endless, mysterious, woods or play golf on the nine-hole course we had constructed in the fields of wild grass. For the "greens" we would just mow the grass very short. We had a sand trap and a briar patch trap and a sixty yard drive for the longest fairway.

My friends and I had an old boat we kept in a swamp. The swamp had a small water passage into a nice sized lake where we would we would go skinny-dipping. We would paddle out to the middle of the lake and dive into the murky water from the boat. That lake was always reddish murky, must have been its connection to the swamp. To keep the boat from leaking we had smeared the hull with liberal amounts of tar. That black tar would be smudged all over us after climbing into the boat a few times. We would paddle around the swamp and would fill the boat with mud turtles while the leeches would slither up the sides of the boat. There were large trees and many plants that grew around the swamp which made it seem very prehistoric and I guess in a sense it was. It was unexplored territory filled with Rattle Snakes and Water moccasin's and in the past, bears, cougars, wolves and other threatening creatures. It was probably that way for thousands of years.

Teenaged me at the house my dad built in Michigan, on M 59

It was the early fifties when our family moved from the garage house to a small house Dad built on M-59, a two lane state highway that crossed Michigan north to south. Mom, Dad and I, with my younger brother Darrell, lived there. My older brother Don, five years my senior, didn't live with us at the time, he had joined the Air Force before we moved to Michigan.

One day I discovered a 78 rpm record my parents had acquired. The record was black and had a red orange label surrounding the hole in the middle.

The words printed around the circular edge read *Good Time Jazz* with the band's name *The Firehouse Five Plus Two*. It was my introduction to Dixieland Jazz, a musical form begun in the late eighteen hundreds. I think I read somewhere that during the civil war there were many morale building military bands which had no use for their instruments after everyone stopped shooting each other. Many of these instruments ended up in New Orleans and the youngsters managed to acquire them and learned to make music. Having no formal musical training allowed them to develop a style peculiar to their own culture. Someone, don't know who, called it Dixieland Jazz, most likely because it originated in the

The Good Time Jazz label

southern United States. Dixie was that area south of the Mason-Dixon Line, the dividing line between the "free" states of the North, and the slave states of the South.

The young musicians of New Orleans were popular enough entertainers that the river boats that worked the big Mississippi River, not only hauling goods but passengers too, would hire them for onboard entertainment. The river boats carried the Dixieland jazz bands and their music from New Orleans up to Chicago and the rest of the world. The home of the band which was featured on this Good Time Jazz record I was holding in my hand was in Burbank, California, a very long way from New Orleans or Michigan. The men of *The Firehouse Five plus Two* were either top artists at Walt Disney Studios or were connected to the Disney Studios in some other capacity. Their love of music had inspired them to learn Dixieland and play the music for fun. By doing so, they had become very successful

Me as a 15 year old

jazz musicians. Interesting to note that people "play" music, musicians don't work music. I don't think anyone would listen to music played by someone who had to work at it and *The Firehouse Five Plus Two* is all playful fun.

I made it to my senior year while attending Waterford Township High School in Michigan. When we first arrived in Michigan I was reluctant to start a new school. It wasn't easy to become part of the gang at that school because most of the kids had known each other forever, since birth, and as for me, having lived in California, I felt like a minority. The majority of those kids had never been to California.

A few kids called me "Hollywood" which for some reason seemed flattering but I think I would have felt closer to them if they would have instead used my name when referring to me. I finally developed some acceptance in my senior year and was elected senior class treasurer. I played basketball in my junior year, got pneumonia half way through the season and had to quit, ending a very short sports career which I wasn't all that good at anyway. I had to spend two weeks in bed and took sulfa drugs in pill form. This must have been before penicillin, which didn't matter, because I later became allergic to it. I guess Mom was right about going out in the cold with wet hair. She was probably right about a lot of things that I later had to learn the hard way.

My young Dad on the left with brother Caleb, sister Amynell and brothers, Finney and Weston.

My father was working with my uncle Weston, my dad's brother, at a Buick agency doing body work. They worked on damaged autos, fixing fender dents and stuff like that. Years later Mother told me Dad had become very upset at the time because there was a black man, Tommy, doing the same job as my dad. Dad found out that Tommy was being paid less than he was and Dad didn't think that was fair. He was very upset about it but either he didn't have the power to change the situation or the guts to quit the job. My parents were tolerant people and never racists but my mother had an exception, she didn't like Mormons. I guess that made her a bigot as far as Mormons were concerned. She said they had trouble telling the truth. Years later I discovered that some people will tell you what they think you want to hear. They want to make you feel good and that can be an honorable thing. I guess some people think it's better for you to feel good than to know the truth. I think my mom thought that was dishonest.

Around October, 1952, my high school senior class went on the annual senior trip to Camp Chief Noonday outside the town of Hastings, Michigan. It was a summer camp with cabins in the woods on the edge of one of the many beautiful Michigan lakes. This trip was the first time I had ever ventured away from home outside the supervision of my parents. I felt very grown up, grown up enough to help a few of the boys throw one of the teachers into the almost-frozen lake. The diminutive female teacher, being less physically threatening than the male teachers, was easier to catch. She was shivering almost violently when she waded out of that lake. Must have of been okay with everyone, though, for there were no reprimands handed out. I think throwing a teacher in the lake was a tradition, fall or summer. Sometimes unreasonable acts can be continued if they fall under the title of "tradition".

My grandmother died that first year we were back in Michigan. I do remember we were still living in that little garage house and I was in that room when my grandmother died. I don't remember her being at the house on M-59. I don't remember the funeral. As a youngster I didn't feel real close to my grandma but I was saddened by her death. People get close and then, by death, or other circumstances, leave each other's presence to never connect again. As I've gotten older I've become more aware of that; friends and lovers so close, so important in the moment, never to be seen again. Makes me wonder how important the people are who are close to me now. Who is close to me now? Someday we may not be close. People fade into one's life and then fade out. All that's left is a graveyard of memories which we occasionally visit in our minds as we recall the good times and the bad.

After Grandma died my parents decided to move back to California. It was just after I had started my senior year in high school. I wonder why my folks decided to move to California this third time and why it was so important to take me out of school in my senior year. I had worked so hard to become accepted by the kids and now we had to leave. My younger brother, Darrell, had just started high school so it couldn't have been too good for him either. Maybe the folks just couldn't take another winter. Maybe my dad lost his job. I hope my dad quit the prejudiced Buick agency instead of getting laid off but I'll never know. I was very happy to be back in the warm California sunshine. Back to Burbank High School with all of the kids I went to school with in junior high. Our family moved into a small, furnished house on Grismer Street in Burbank, next door to a school buddy of mine, Vernon Gregory. I remember the dining room table in the house had a kind of a light green marbled looking Formica top and chrome legs. I'd apparently developed some sense of taste by this time for it just looked cheap to me. I think I realized then that we were not well off. When do kids become aware of these things?

Most of my friends had become beer drinkers and smokers. My buddy, Vernon, became the senior class treasurer, the same position I had held in my senior year in Michigan, by odd coincidence. A thin guy, he liked to drink excessive amounts of beer and smoke cigarettes, as we all did. Before the end of that year he quit smoking and started lifting weights. He became very muscular and proud of his physique. He was a new man.

I was happy to be back in California and happy to land a new part time job with my friend Danny Ludwig in a "burr shop" making a dollar thirty an hour. We would clean small aircraft parts free of sharp metal splinters called "burrs" to make them smooth. The shop was on Victory Boulevard in Burbank and was owned by Mr. White. Danny worked there and put in a good word for me so I got the job.

A few of the guys in high school had custom cars. "Frenchie" owned a "lowered," 1939 customized convertible Mercury, with a grey primer finish and a dashboard with twenty coats of black lacquer. He invited me to ditch school one day so he could show off his car while he gave me a tour of L.A. We drove with the top down and I ended up with enough of a sunburn to cause my mother to know that I had not been in school that day. She only commented on my sunburn but didn't pry.

My grades were okay that senior year so I graduated from Burbank High in June, 1953. We had the commencement exercise at John Burroughs High School which had been converted to a high school from the junior high I had attended in the seventh grade. We had the graduation ceremony at Stough Park in the hills of Burbank. It was a wonderful time but my mother wasn't there. Neither was my dad. My mother had developed some sort of depression and was severely detached from participating in the reality of daily life. My dad had put her in a hospital in Los Angeles. I don't know why my dad wasn't at my graduation; maybe he was visiting my mother. She was depressed enough that they gave her "Electro Shock" therapy. Tough treatment, "Don't dare be depressed or we'll electrocute you again." We have anti-depressant drugs today, but some doctors still use Electro Shock therapy. Now it's called Electroconvulsive Therapy, yeah that's better. It was and is pretty cruel and crude. I think my mother got depressed because my dad had taken on a real estate deal which she was opposed to. The longer he worked on it the sicker she got until he had to give up the deal to take care of her. I don't know where he got the money to do either one. He finally gave up the real estate deal and Mother finally got well. How powerful the mind.

Me and my buddy, Vern Gregory

After graduation, Vern Gregory, my self and another friend decided to go to Northern California and become lumberjacks for the summer. I had applied for a scholarship at The Art Center School in Los Angeles but the dean told me I should get a summer job, save my money and come back in the fall. That was his way of saying "you aren't good enough for a scholarship". My friends and I had heard that lumberjacks made a lot of money. We headed North in Vern's powder blue 1941 Chevy. When we got to Eureka, we rented an apartment and went to the store and bought canned beans and beer. Then we headed to the local lumber company to become lumberjacks. We were told it had been a very rainy wet spring and the lumber business was in a slump. On the way back to the apartment we saw the line around the employment office. Seemed there were a lot of jacks with no lumber. We should have learned from that experience to always check ahead. I guess no one taught us that in high school or we weren't listening. To add to our problems the elderly lady who had rented us the apartment had second thoughts about three beer-drinking, bean-eating, teenage boys, living in her apartment. She told us we would have to leave. She told us that her son was unexpectedly coming into town and she would need the apartment. I think it was the third day in Eureka when we realized that the lumberjack business wasn't going to work for us so we decided to head back South. One of the guys stayed on, ran out of money, and was later arrested for vagrancy. His dad had to come up and bail him out of jail. Vern and I got home before our mail arrived, the postcards we had sent to our folks from Eureka.

With that inglorious educational beginning of my life after high school, I started looking for a job in Burbank. I found one at a company which manufactured big portable backyard barbecues. My job was to take the big iron barbecue dish part off an overhead moving track and dip it in a big vat of black paint which was sunken into the floor. Then I would lift the part up, dripping with black paint, and hook it back on the moving track. It was an evening job. I started at four o'clock in the afternoon and worked until twelve midnight. By the time I left work at midnight I was covered in black paint down to my shoes. I wondered why they didn't have the track move down so the part automatically dipped into the paint and out again with a newly painted part, saving the little money they paid me. The only good thing about the job was that I had afternoons to look for another job.

I found a day job at an army surplus store on Victory Boulevard and quit the job at the midnight black paint mess. At my new job I was either working outside, where it was very hot, or in a big warehouse without air conditioning which was hotter than it was outside. When we worked in the warehouse one of our jobs was burning out the sizes of surplus army boots with a soldering iron and stamping them with a different size. Don't know why we did that. Another chore involved filling up, with alcohol, old partially-evaporated bottles of army surplus hair tonic. Sometimes I worked outside. It was one hundred twelve degrees in the shade that summer. We topped off half-empty fire extinguishers with a chemical called carbon tetrachloride. The guy I worked with, an ex- marine, got sick and went to the hospital with what the doctors at first thought was pneumonia. Then they thought he had polio. It turned out he had inhaled too much "carbon tet". I never saw him again after that. My Mother always told me I had weak lungs but the ex-marine got sick and I survived. I think my mother thought that I had weak lungs because of the bout with pneumonia that ruined my basketball career in high school.

That summer I struggled through my job at the army surplus store looking forward to art school and what that new life would bring. My summer earnings nest egg would help for the purchase of art supplies which I would later find out were astronomically priced. A sheet of water color paper, one sheet, three dollars! A water color brush, one brush, would cost twelve dollars! I was venturing into a new financial dynamic. My dad was going to pay my tuition and I would be investing my meager summer job savings in a future which was at the moment a construction in my head, a dream.

CHAPTER 2
Learning with the Pros

I enrolled at The Art Center School of Los Angeles, the fall of 1953. Dad bought a used, thirteen year old, 1940 Ford Deluxe Convertible for me so I could get to school over on 5353 West Third Street in Los Angeles.

I still wonder how he could have afforded my tuition and the car. We were living on Babcock Street off Victory Boulevard in North Hollywood, so it was a bit of a haul to The Art Center School and I needed a car. Public transportation was out of the question because of the distance. I was the third owner of that car. It was a thirteen year old car but it had new naugahyde upholstery. It was almost like new except for a few primer spots here and there and a worn out top. I received the original sales papers which stated the cost of the car new was $750 and my dad paid $200 for it. I polished the firewall, had a new white convertible top added to replace the old one, and dressed up the engine with chrome accessories. I put motorcycle tires on the front and Cadillac tires on the rear to give it that nose down "rake" look. I was very happy. I had a car with a rake.

Starting art school was a jolting experience. All of the instructors were professionals with long careers in their

A 1940 Ford convertible like the one I owned

chosen fields and very knowledgeable, not only at their specialty, but very experienced in the world of business. And to make my new school experience even more intimidating were the students who had fought in the Korean War. They seemed much more grown up than the high school kids I was used to. I guess because they had been shot at, an experience which would make anyone more serious. I was eighteen years old and these "vets" were in their mid twenties or older and serious about their schooling. I was learning words like cantilever, digression, and tangent. Of course I felt very ignorant and foolish for not knowing all of the stuff I had come to school to learn.

I purchased my first art supplies with the money I had saved over the summer and was fortunate enough to get a job cleaning classrooms and emptying the trash in the lavatories after school and Saturdays. I was paid 90 cents an hour for that job. The next semester I found a job which paid more, a job in a machine shop in Burbank. It was in a building behind the shop owner's house. In the front room of the building the boss tended to his first love. He had a recording studio where he recorded square dance music. I would work at night and Saturdays and would operate, if I wasn't very careful, a hand splattering punch press which stamped out metal parts for things. Or I would operate what was called an OD grinder, OD for outside dimension. That one was used for grinding down long rods to make them fit in things; in our case, we were making car radio antennas. I would carefully lay a metal rod into the machine and if things worked correctly out would come a smaller rod of just the right size for the telescoping radio antenna. Why didn't they just buy rods which were the right size to begin with? If things didn't go correctly for me and that machine, out would fly a wire projectile with skull piercing force. I was very scared and very careful around that machine and fortunately was never afforded the opportunity to see it angry.

Some evenings I would just sit and drill holes into the little metal balls that they used to fit on top of the radio antenna. I would put the little brass ball in a device which held it tight so it wouldn't turn when the drill was drilling. Many machines of this nature had oil running on the part you were drilling so as to keep it cool. The machine I used had no cooling system. As I was drilling, the very hot metal fragments would come out of the little ball and rest on the hand I was using to hold the device. I couldn't wear gloves because gloves made it too difficult to pick up the little brass balls. So I would experiment to see if I could force my mind to not feel the burning sensation. I could drill more little balls faster if I didn't have to stop and recover from the painful burning fragments piled on my hand. No matter how far detached from reality I tried to force my mind to be, the reality was that the metal fragments still burned my hand, so much for mind over matter.

The next year I found a better job in a fiber glass auto shop, Victress Auto

Body in Van Nuys. A couple of young guys who had majored in auto design at The Art Center School had started a business making fiberglass sports car bodies of their own design. When they hired me the company was not yet profitable so they sacrificed by paying themselves a third of what they paid me, which was a $1.50 an hour. They worked from early morn to late evening and weekends. They were Dedicated with a capital D. I wonder where those guys are now. I hope they're doing well. We also made full-sized plaster auto models. We layered sheets of resin soaked fiberglass in the molds to create the sports car bodies they sold. Working after school and weekends, trying to keep up with my school homework assignments, and attempts to visit with my new girlfriend Judy, made me a busy boy, a busy boy with declining grades at The Art Center School.

At the end of my second year of art school I was ask by the Ford Motor Company, along with nine other promising students of automobile design, to work through the summer of 1955 in the new design studio of Lincoln Continental in Dearborn, Michigan. The Ford Motor Company gave us each two hundred dollars and told us to fly to Detroit; it would be my first time in an airplane. My art school buddy, Bob Elder, was also invited, so we boarded a DC-7 at the Los Angeles International Airport for an eight-hour red-eye flight to Detroit. Jet aircraft had not yet become the favored mode of air travel in 1955 so we had to suffer the long flight in a noisy propeller driven aircraft, a "prop job". That first flight did instill in me a need to be confident that no matter how frightened I became the plane would stay airborne. After a couple hours in the air my buddy Bob looked out a window and alerted me to a huge, blue and yellow flame being projected from one of the engines. We were totally alarmed but of course being amateur flyers we wanted to look brave and courageous. No one else on the aircraft seemed disturbed that the airplane we were in, flying over the western desert in the middle of the night, looked very much like it was going to go down in flames. Bob and I decided since no one else seemed worried it would be okay to go down in flames and we would be brave about it. We sat back in our seats and eventually fell asleep.

When I awoke I was relieved to still be in the air without any fire spewing from the engine and the sunlight pouring though the windows. In the light I could clearly see that the stewardess, who just said good morning as she walked by, was probably a bit older than I and very attractive. I was a very embarrassed, disheveled, nineteen year old having just awakened after sleeping in my nifty dark blue suit with pleated pants. I was in no condition to be viewed by a cute "stewdy". I was trying very hard to be grownup, trying to press the wrinkles out of my suit and hide any evidence of my nineteen year old manliness. I sat up straight, made a serious attempt to appear gentlemanly, and muttered a "good morning".

It was my first experience to view the world from such a height in the daylight when we arrived over Michigan. It was a very pleasant view for everything looked miniature, well-crafted, and model-like. All clean and tidy, unlike the close up look one has standing at ground level where debris and decay are in sharper focus.

A few of my Michigan cousins, L to R Marynell, Elizabeth, CE and Sam

Most of my relatives still lived in Michigan so Bob and I were met at the airport by a group of my cousins. After all of the intros and hellos we were off to a cousin's house to gather in the back yard to relax and catch up on our experiences. After chatting for awhile everyone, almost zombie like, got up and started for the house. The sun was beginning to set and the group exodus confused me so I ask what was happening. Everyone in a random response uttered one word: "mosquitoes". Yes, the evening in the good old Michigan summertime was owned by an insect. After living in California for a few years I had forgotten what a nuisance that bug can be.

We were invited to stay at my cousin's house. Marynell and her husband Ed were so kind as to put us up until we could find an apartment. And Ed was generous enough to loan us his car so we would have a way to get to our jobs at Ford. The morning we were to report to work was as exciting as surviving our first flight across the U.S. We were met in the lobby of the new design studio by the men who were the left and right hand men of the Chief Stylist, John M. Reinhart. We were going to help design the newest version of the Lincoln Continental in the new Continental design center. Talk about inflated teenaged egos. The Continental was the luxury auto of the early forties which Ford hoped to bring back in the late fifties. It was a great summer, new Lincoln autos at our disposal, which we could drive to lunch and dinner, plus lots of overtime, which meant big bucks for a young teenager. It was my second time living away from home, the first being that senior class trip. But this time I had to be an adult, which meant grown up freedom. Pool halls, pizza, beer, Bill Haley's *Rock Around The Clock,* and the first issue of *Playboy Magazine,* it was the good times.

Bob and I rented a single furnished apartment which was closer to work. It had two single beds in the living room. We didn't have sheets or blankets so we just slept on the mattress in our jeans. We didn't even think of buying sheets or blankets but we bought a very used Ford to get around in, we now felt self-sufficient. During that summer I came to the conclusion that I had been spoiled by the California sunshine. The good times in Michigan were too often spoiled by gloomy, lightning-struck, rainy, stormy, and windy, very humid, insect-filled days. Lousy weather invaded too many summer afternoons, blew down the trees, flooded the streets and made life generally miserable. The natives like to say, "if you don't like the weather here, stick around a minute and it'll change." They were right but I didn't want to stick around much less live there forever. California had spoiled me.

After that productive summer of 1955, as designer and sculptor, Ford eventually produced the car we had help design. It was called the 1958 Mark IV Continental. Well, helped design might be a stretch since I mostly sculpted what had been designed by the senior designer guys. We worked on full size clay models, each side of a different design idea. We would finish the model and then clean up the studio for a showing. At the appointed time in would come a bunch of executives led by William Clay Ford, son of Edsel Ford. William Clay was head of the Continental Division at the time. We would move off to the background and listen to their crit.

We finished our summer of work at Ford, the automobile design for the Continental Mark IV was completed, and I was flattered at the exit interview when the Ford Motor Company representative asked me if I would return to work with Ford if asked, and of course I said yes. With my ego inflated I headed back to California. I landed in L.A. with my fifth semester of The Art Center School looming ahead. Ford never called but if they had called I would have been faced with the decision of choosing whether to live in Michigan or California. That would have been difficult.

Back in California The Art Center School had become The Art Center College of Design, it wasn't just an art school anymore, it was a college. The school had become accredited and I had to take the academic classes which I had missed in high school. Having a social life and working part time began to have serious adverse effects on my grades. It was very difficult to stay awake during those academic classes for they were Saturday lecture classes of the most boring subjects, such as Business and English. I did get a good grade in both my English class and the Art History class for I wrote an essay for Art History that I also submitted to my English class as my term paper. I received and an A in Art History and a B+ in English. But the effort to attend school six days a week, do all of my homework, work two or three hours a night and Saturday after school at a part time job was tough enough, but I was trying to have a social life too.

The time with my girlfriend Judy meant time away from my homework, which was considerable. But I shouldn't whine. I was comfortably living at home in my own studio bedroom while my friend Bob, from Florida, was living in an office space which he paid for with his labor as a janitor in the building, and still going to school during the day. He was living on peanut butter sandwiches except for one night a week when he ate at an Italian restaurant. The restaurant had an all you could eat spaghetti night and Bob would go a few days without eating and then on the "all you can eat night" he would try to eat enough so he wouldn't get hungry for a few days. He was eating so much spaghetti that the restaurant started adding hot spice to his pasta so he wouldn't be able to eat it. He had to quit dining there but that didn't stop him, he continued his schooling.

A youthful Judy

It was my fifth semester of art school and after two and a half years I was beginning to lose my drive. I was anxious to get on with my life. My girlfriend, Judy, and I wanted to get married; well, she wanted to get married to get out from under the oppression of her parents. I wanted to get married to keep her happy and that would make me happy. Getting married meant that I would need an income greater than my part time jobs which helped pay for school. My grades were slipping and there was a point when the dean was concerned enough to call me into her office and to tell me that I needed a "mental kick in the pants". That didn't seem to help so I decided to quit school. I thought it would be less degrading if I took charge and quit school before the dean had a chance to throw me out. There is still a place in my psyche where quitting art school without a degree has the weight of failure. It was failure, an ending, but it was also a new beginning.

CHAPTER 3
Walt Disney Wants Me

After struggling through five semesters at The Art Center College of Design in Los Angeles, California, I, at the age of twenty one, decided it was time to conquer the real world. I quit school and threw myself on the job market. Nobody seemed to notice so I acted on some info which came my way. I managed an interview with an industrial design firm in Pasadena. On the appointed day I packed up my portfolio of my best art pieces and headed for Pasadena. I was very nervous during the interview, hands wet, and shaking, all of it. I didn't do very well in that interview and never heard from that company again. A few months later I heard that the guy I interviewed with had committed suicide. I learned a couple of things from that experience. First, the greater your desire to have something the more power you give to those who have that something, and the weaker you make yourself. Who wants to hire a weak person? The more I wanted something the more nervous I was about having it. And number two, the person sitting across the desk from you could be a bigger mess than you are. I really didn't think I was objectionable enough in that interview to cause anyone to commit suicide. Gee, I might have been able to help him if I had not allowed him to have all of the power in that interview.

On Friday, January 13, 1956, Judy and I got married in the Little Brown Church in the San Fernando Valley. A church of some fame, on Coldwater Canyon in Studio City, Ronald Reagan and Nancy were married there on March 4, 1952. That neighborhood has become big and busy but the little church is still there.

The Little Brown Church

Judy made all of the arrangements with the minister a few days before we were to be married so on our appointed date we drove over to the church for the evenings big event. It was just Judy and I with the minister and his daughter as a witness. After taking care of business in the minister's office he instructed us to go to the front door of the church and walk down the aisle to the altar, where he would be standing. I don't remember how we were dressed that night but we must have been a cute couple. We walked down the isle to the waiting minister and he performed our little ceremony. After we were married we thanked the minister and told him how wonderful it was. We then, hand in hand, went to an Italian restaurant on Victory Boulevard and had a pizza, just the two of us. Silly kids thinking that being married meant we were all grown up and ready to face the world.

Judy and I started our married life living in my room at my parents' house. My room was behind the garage and served as bedroom and studio. We eventually moved to our first apartment in Burbank. That apartment had a swimming pool so we thought we had arrived at the good life. Judy was much more grown up than I was so she was the one that kept us on an adult track; nice apartment, furniture, civilized things. Women tend to be the keepers of civilization. If one looks around the world at those cultures where the men are in control and keep the women subservient you are most likely to see a chaotic uncivil culture of fear, pain and violence. Judy and I had a civil relationship and I was happy that she was responsible and adult. She started working as a bank teller at Surety Bond Savings and Loan up in Burbank. Fortunately for me I had heard Walt Disney Productions was looking for artists to help do an animated film with the title, *Sleeping Beauty*. As a young man I had automobiles on my mind and had never considered cartoon animation as a career. I wanted to be an automobile designer but that would have meant living in Michigan, which I didn't want to do after having lived there that prior summer. It would still be twenty or thirty years before Detroit moved some of their auto design studios to California where the hot rod car hobbyist of the 40's and 50's had helped change the direction of auto design.

I was very excited about the possibility of working with Walt Disney Productions so I made an appointment to show my portfolio. On that magic day I nervously carted my portfolio to the main gate of Walt Disney Productions. Taking a few deep breaths, shoulders back, chest out, attempting great stage presence,

I followed the signs

I announced my arrival to the guard. He gave me proper directions to my meeting place, Andy Engman's office in the animation building.

"Follow the street signs, Mickey Avenue to Dopey Drive, turn right and enter the animation building on your left. Andy's office would be the first door on your left as you enter the animation building". Got it!

My destination, the animation building

The Disney studio was beautiful. Well-kept buildings, large manicured trees, fearless, frisky squirrels scampering across green grassy lawns edged with colorful flowers, and busy people scurrying everywhere! I felt very special walking up Mickey Avenue, frightened, nervous and beatific. I found Mr. Engman's office and told the secretary who I was and she introduced me to Andy. Everybody was on a first name basis at the studio, an informality that relaxed me. Andy was a little overweight, sweet, kind of gruff guy who had been a character animator at Disney's for years. He had moved into the effects department and later into a middle management position. He was a studio veteran. In those days a lot of the guys were tough, heavy drinking party guys. Not sure why unless it was just tough to hang on to a job as an artist or maybe they were just fun guys.

After my portfolio was perused by Andy, Johnny Bond, a Disney animation fixture for many years and drinking buddy of Andy's, gave me an In-between Test. The test consisted of me doing a drawing of Donald Duck, which fit precisely between two other drawings of Donald Duck, unfortunately for me each duck drawing was in a different position. This forced my drawing to be a different duck than the other two. Yikes. The duck drawings had been drawn by somebody who knew how to draw Donald Duck. I had never tried to draw Donald Duck. I had drawn autos, airplanes, wrenches, carburetors, girls, but never a famous duck or even a regular duck. I wasn't too nervous but I didn't know what I was doing, I didn't understand the concept of animation. When the drawings were viewed in sequence, Donald Duck magically came to life. Ah, the magic of animation! Pencil drawings come to life, I was hooked. I also did the same test but with drawings of clouds. I had no idea what was expected. I went home and anxiously awaited a response to what was my Herculean effort to impress Andy Engman and Johnny Bond. Fortunately for me, the studio needed effects artists. A few days later I received a call from Andy's secretary asking me to report to the studio as a trainee in the animation effects department. I was thrilled. Having just gotten married it was comforting to know I was a responsible husband and would be working as a professional artist.

In late January I began a thirty-day training program for about $42 a week. I had never considered animation as a career but I was impressed enough by Disney's *Pinocchio* to make sure I was smart enough never to be turned into a donkey by some creepy guy with a wagon pulled by donkeys who were once gullible little boys. During my orientation tour of the studio the lady in charge said to the group that we would all be driving Cadillac's in ten years. I was driving a Volkswagen ten years later, but it was a "brand new" Volkswagen. Oddly enough, ten years later, I was out in the real world of Culver City working on technical films. I had resigned from Disney to accept a job offer which I thought would propel me to even greater heights, but back to *Sleeping Beauty*.

During my training period I worked on a few short films: *Paul Bunyan, Wind Wagon Smith* and *Our Friend the Atom*, polishing my skills for the feature we would soon be working on. I couldn't believe they were paying me to do this stuff. I was doodling for dollars! I was working with the likes of Jack Boyd, Art Stevens, Cliff Nordberg, Ed Parks, all old timers in the animation business. When I started on the short films, Josh Meador, one of the old time effects animators, was the department supervisor. He was a successful master

My first year as an artist for Walt Disney

painter with an art gallery in Carmel. He said his wife was running the gallery and "she sells everything I paint". While chatting with a few of us he told us that one day he found himself in his room reading the paper all day, it occurred to him that he hadn't had an assignment from Walt for a while. In doing some detective work he found that he had somehow crossed Walt and was on Walt's bad side. Maybe that was the time he had told Walt, "I could complete a short by myself in less time than it would take a whole studio crew to do it." Josh was a hard working artist. Eventually all was worked out and Josh was back to his projects. In between projects he was taking six month painting sabbaticals to sketch landscapes for painting reference. Josh had animated effects on many Disney movies: among the many was *Snow White and the Seven Dwarfs, Pinocchio, Dumbo, Bambi,* even up to *Sleeping Beauty*. He was always willing to crit my sketches and to share his talent with positive reinforcement of my efforts. At the time I really didn't grasp the value of such a privilege, to have a very successful artist sharing their expertise with me.

After a period of working on the shorts I was assigned to *Sleeping Beauty*. Ah, a real animated feature to work on. My very first Walt Disney feature! I was eventually promoted to assistant animator working with Jack Buckley, a master effects animator and painter who had started at the studio in the late forties.

Jack Buckley, the last time we got together

I was working with famous artists who had

25

created successful lives in the animation business. My days were filled with drawing pixie dust, burning thorn bushes, and flapping fairy wings. I kept a notepad taped to my desk and to take a break I would draw a race car on the last page, and then, on the preceding pages I would draw the car in progressive stages of crashing. I would then flip the pages and the car would appear to race to a fiery finish. Drawings come to life. Sometimes my fun would be interrupted by a seething Jack storming into the room, slinging a packet of his scene across the room after a meeting with a loud, rude, cursing, cigar-smoking, Clyde Geronomi, the movies director. I had heard that Clyde used an abundance of four letter words with a force which could remove wallpaper. Of course I heard this from Jack; as an assistant animator I never had my own experience with that force. Jack animated most of the pixie dust in the film. No particle systems in those days, we were the particle system! I thought it would take the rest of my life doing the assistant work on the sequence where the fairies put the castle to sleep, but it did look magical when it was finished. The picture was shot in the Super Technirama 70 Cinematographic Process which is a name about as long as the cinemascope paper we had to draw the animation on. The paper we used was more than twice as wide as the paper for standard 35 millimeter movies. Holding up that paper to flip the drawings all day required an athletic ability. My left arm is still bigger than my right arm.

In the sequence where the fire breathing dragon sets the thorn forest ablaze in her attempt to fry the prince, Jack animated the fire. He decided to use orange and yellow pastel chalks. I was never a fan of pastels simply because I could do a nice still life with them but I ended up with more chalk on me than my art. Drawing fire with those pastel chalks on those big sheets of paper caused me to realize I was no longer doodling for dollars but rather laboring for love, the love I had for pencils and standard sized paper. I was very happy to get back to at least drawing with pencils when we animated the thorn forest while the prince sliced through it with his trusty sword. But of course we still had to do it on that big paper. Jack liked my work so well he gave me a chance to animate, to test my mettle. I was to animate the effects in a scene, a long shot, where the angry fog of doom envelopes the castle. I did so well on that scene that Jack let me animate the bridge collapsing, when the Prince, on his horse, jumps the castle's moat.

In those days smoking cigarettes, cigars, or a pipe for the more erudite was a socially acceptable way of doing yourself in with a horrible disease while thinking it was a marvelous pastime. Almost every one smoked, in their cars, in their home, at work, while dining; there were even water-proof cigarettes. Those were great for people who wanted to smoke while they showered. I smoked in all of those places except the shower. I smoked at work, in the building, in my car, at my desk, in my home, very stinky. Jack smoked cigars and me, cigarettes. I had an ashtray which was usually filled to the smelly brim with fumatorious debris but Jack refused to use an ashtray; instead he would lay his lit cigar on the edge of his desk drawer. One afternoon I was feverishly flapping those big sheets of paper while drawing fire with orange and yellow colored chalk when I heard Jack rustling about. I looked over to see my flames rising out of Jack's waste basket. I'm drawing fire so well that its' coming out of Jack's waste basket? Jack hurriedly slid his flaming waste basket, which his cigar had fallen into, my way, his face glowing from the bright fire swirling into the air. I'd swear he had a mischievous look of glee as the waste basket left a trail of smoke and flames rising high in the air as it slid toward me. I jumped up and stopped the burning basket before it arrived under the water sprinkler, which protruded from the ceiling, just above my head. By this time Jack had composed himself enough to grab a piece of chip board to place over the fire, smothering it. We always worked with our door closed and in a few minutes we heard people out in the hallway shuffling about and muttering about the smell of smoke. Jack and I furiously fanned the smoke with chip boards and waited a few minutes for the smell of smoke to clear our room. We then opened the door to see the studio fire marshal and a bunch of people milling about in the hallway. They all had their noses in the air sniffing like dogs on the trail of drug smugglers, everyone announcing the smell of smoke as if they were in the chorus of a Broadway musical, "Yes, I smell smoke, we all smell smoke, yes, we all smell smoke." Jack and I joined them sniffing with our noses in the air, more convinced than any of them that we smelled smoke. Eventually, everyone sniffed all of the smoke out of the air and the smell went away, as did the fire marshal and all of the worried people. Jack and I went back in our room, closed the door and snickered quietly while we continued to work, relieved that we didn't burn down the studio while animating fire on those big sheets of paper. An L.A. Times headline, "Disney animator with large left arm sets studio ablaze with his big paper fired fury." Years later, New Years Eve, midnight 1977, I quit smoking for good. I decided after smoking for twenty six years I should be the master in charge of me and stop the unhealthy habit.

Occasionally I would receive an invitation to an ARI, an Audience Reaction Interview for a new film or TV show which was being screened in one of the animation studio's many small screening rooms called sweat boxes. The term sweat box came about because in the early days the animators would show Walt Disney their work in those screening rooms and there would be a lot of nervous sweating in anticipation of Walt's comments. The ARI screenings would be a chance for an audience to submit comments about the film they just saw, hopefully improving the film.

During the lunch breaks we could go to the sound stages and watch a live action production being filmed. The sound stages weren't so secure in those days, to my benefit. Standing quietly in the dark, I'd watch all of the stagehands, electricians, actors and actresses while photographing a real movie scene. It was a super experience. Sometimes I would find out where *The Firehouse Five plus Two* was rehearsing. That experience was a fantasy comes to life, for I had discovered the group on that record in Michigan years earlier. I would take my brown bag and sit in an audience of maybe two or three people. Ward Kimball, the band's leader, always welcomed us, apparently glad to have fans listen. Yes, they were still working at Disney when I started at the studio in 1956 and were more popular than ever. They even played at the opening of Disneyland the year before. I will always remember Ward Kimball's snappy outfits. He would wear bright colors and not be concerned with subtleties. He would wear a red shirt, yellow tie, blue pants with green suspenders and a nifty hat of any color or any combo of colors depending on the day. Ward Kimball, the only Disney artist Walt ever called a genius, started the band after he taught himself to play the trombone. Frank Thomas played piano. Both were members of the "Nine Old Men", Walt's key group of animators. To this day I listen to the Fire House Five CD's in my home and in my car, so happy that technology allows us to preserve our favorites of the past. I was twenty one years old and thought I was accomplished, privileged, and there was no where to go but up! Those were good days. The Mickey Mouse Club was thriving and I would see the Mousketeers and Annette Funicello bouncing around the studio. I would see Cliff Edwards driving his Nash, an automobile that ceased production years ago, on to the studio lot. His name was painted on his spare tire cover with a picture of Pinocchio at the center.

In those days, European sports cars were the rage, so I bought a British sports car, a 1956 Austin Healy.

The body paint was a Robin's egg blue and that didn't work for me, too sweet. I wanted more of a Ferrari Red. My dad volunteered to paint it for me so we spent a few days turning my little Austin Healy into a hot red machine. I loved that car almost as much as I loved my job at Walt Disney Productions almost as much as I loved my wife Judy. I had a lot to love and a still much more to learn.

My 1956 Austin Healy and me

I'm sure at one time or another we all wonder why, when things are so good, the good times must end.

Judy and I lived in Burbank at this time. We had left our place with the swimming pool because we thought we could save money if we rented a completely unfurnished place and buy our own furniture. We rented a small one bedroom apartment on Riverside Drive, just down from the Disney studio and went furniture shopping. After we settled in, our work day would begin with Judy driving us to the studio in my sports car and then she would continue on up to Burbank, for her teller job. Judy and I were making more money so of course it was time to get a bigger, more comfortable, apartment. We moved to an apartment on Oak Street, across the street from Columbia Studios. Gee, we moved a lot. About the time I thought I was on top of the world I received my first lesson in taking things for granted and good times ending. Good times not just ending but coming to a screeching halt.

We had only lived in that apartment a month or so when I sat down one evening to sort through the day's mail. I came across a letter from the President of The United States which began with, "Greetings from the President of the United States." Wow, I was doing such a good job at the studio on *Sleeping Beauty* that President Eisenhower was writing to praise me. No, the letter turned out to be a request from President Eisenhower for me to report to the United States Army Infantry at Fort Ord California. I was to serve two years learning to be a soldier, defending our country from whatever enemies we might face. I thought my career was just taking off and now the President wanted me to put it on hold, leave my wife and my sports car, and be a soldier

Year 1957, working on my sports car with my wife Judy

in the U.S. Army. I wasn't finished with *Sleeping Beauty,* my career in cartoon animation, or my wife Judy.

We had signed a lease for the apartment and thought we would be there without interruption but President Eisenhower thought differently. So did the apartment manager. He wasn't concerned the least bit that I had been called to serve with the military to protect his apartment building from being overrun by an evil force. He refused to refund our security deposit or our last month's rent, nothing.

CHAPTER 4

Uncle Sam Wants Me Too!

I survived my military physical examination in downtown Los Angeles and later reported to the Union Station to travel by train to Fort Ord near Monterey. I would be there for eight weeks of basic military infantry training. I left Judy to live with my mom and dad but it was my mother who cried when I said good bye. I always wondered why she was crying when it was me that was being forced to go away from my nice life for two years. Mom's love blossomed for she was worried about me.

I learned to be a real good soldier in those eight weeks but the Army thought I needed another eight weeks of training so I would be a really good soldier. After completion of the eight weeks at Fort Ord, those military folks sent me to Fort Carson, outside of Colorado Springs, Colorado, for eight weeks of advance infantry training. I no longer had control of the trajectory for my life and felt like a leaf blowing in the wind, the wind being the U.S. Army. Fortunately it was springtime in Colorado so there was no snow but every afternoon there would be a thunderstorm. It would usually catch us out in the field playing war. The thunder, lightning, hail, wind, rain, was lousy weather to be out in.

During my stay at Fort Carson, I noticed a soft bump, about the size of a large vitamin capsule cut in half, in my right groin area. Each night when I would lie down on my bunk bed it would seem a little larger than the day before. I could push on it and it would go away but as soon as I started to get up it would pop out again. I had no idea what it was but I knew if I went on sick call and it turned out to be something serious it would set back my training and who knows where I would go after that.

I received orders about that time and gee whiz, they were going to send

31

me to Hawaii after I finished my advance infantry training. Now for certain I couldn't go on sick call. For sure if I had to leave my outfit and go have surgery they would later send me to some God forsaken place like Alaska or worse. Maybe they would send me to Korea, so I could help make sure the Korean War wouldn't flare up again. The bump kept getting bigger but there was no pain. By this time it was about the size of an egg on the right side just above my groin. I kept soldiering on hoping my egg wouldn't hatch, not knowing for sure what alien creature it might be. I finally finished that grueling eight weeks of advanced infantry training. I now knew how to throw grenades, fight close combat with a bayonet on my rifle, shoot a Browning Automatic Rifle, sleep out in the rain, fire a 106 millimeter recoilless rifle, one of those big guns they used to mount on a jeep and I learned to fire 30 caliber machine guns and pistols. The Army wanted me bad.

After my eight weeks of training the Army decided I knew enough about all of that stuff so they put me on a bus to the Denver Colorado train station for a train ride to Los Angeles, by way of Salt Lake City, Utah. I got to spend a few days at home in North Hollywood with my wife and family before heading for Travis Air Force Base outside of Oakland. I was to wait there for a flight to Hawaii with MATS, the Military Air Transport Service. I guess I wasn't smart enough at the time or was afraid to find out what this strange funny goose egg size bump was doing on my lower right groin area. I was hauling around a sixty pound duffle bag but had no idea that a strain could pop this thing open, I hadn't read the literature yet. We didn't have Google in those days. At Travis we had nothing to do but wait for a flight to Hawaii. We shot pool, went to the movies, ate in the Air Force mess and checked in every morning and afternoon at the airport desk to see if there were any flights to Hawaii. I was on vacation from my Army infantry training.

It was a couple of weeks of hanging out with the Air Force before I caught an evening flight in a Boeing Stratocruiser, another "prop job".

That air craft took eight noisy, dark, night time hours of flying to get across that big Pacific Ocean to land on the island of Oahu, home of the volcano called Diamond Head, and home of Pearl Harbor and Hickam Air Force Base. It was early morning when we landed, before the sun was up. I exited the aircraft and walked out into the dark, flower scented, balmy night air of Hawaii. Off in the dark night I could hear the waves of the great Pacific Ocean washing up on the shore. Even in the dark I could tell Hawaii was beautiful. As I stood there, languid in the flower scented Hawaiian dark, a shout to board the trucks waiting for us brought me back to reality, back to my army duty. We clamored into the back of the trucks and begin a ride which bumped and rolled over and up and over hills which I couldn't see. Eventually we were transported to a military installation and were assigned

My Boeing Stratocruiser, B377 model

to the transient barracks at the infamous Schofield Barracks. I thought it was infamous. At least we had a roof over our heads and bunks to sleep in with clean sheets.

The bump in my groin was still there but I wanted to wait until I was assigned to a regular Army outfit before I went on sick call. It had been about six weeks since I first noticed the bump and it wasn't getting any smaller. In fact it was getting larger! But I didn't want to alter the course which the army had set out for me for fear of being spun into a future of uncertainty. Me and a few other guys assigned there in the transient barracks spent our days playing black jack, exchanging enormous sums of imaginary money, and wondering if the Army had forgotten us. Eventually I was assigned to Company B of the Twenty Fifth Infantry Division of the U.S. Army at Schofield Barracks. Scary! I remembered seeing the movie *From Here to Eternity* with Burt Lancaster and Frank Sinatra. There were many scenes in that movie of the army life at Schofield Barracks and now it was me there. I was assigned to the weapons platoon made up of the 81 mm mortar guys and the 106 mm recoilless rifle guys. Sergeant Domai, a wily little U.S. Army combat veteran of Japanese descent was the platoon sergeant.

As soon as I knew what the army had in mind for me I promptly went on sick call with my egg. Sergeant Domai was convinced that I was a gold bricker, a bug out. He thought I was faking illness. I was sent to Tripler Army Hospital in the hills above Honolulu where the surgeons fixed my goose egg. It turned out to be a right inguinal hernia and it was no fun having half a dozen doctors examining me over a period of a couple days. I guess that was part of their training. I discovered a report which read that the number one cause of death of African males living in the bush was strangulated hernia. It's when a strain forces your intestines to slip though a crack in your lower abdominal region and then gets pinched, cutting off the blood. Ouch! Then Gangrene sets in and in twenty minutes you're dead. I would have been terrified to have had that information before the surgery after hauling that sixty-five pound duffle bag all over the place. I would have been on sick call instantly and probably missed my chance to go to Hawaii. I was relieved to know I was repaired and not in Korea. I spent three weeks in that hospital. The army wouldn't let me go back to play war until I was completely healed.

Well, life wasn't bad. I was staying in a beautiful hospital. It was twelve stories high on the downward side of the mountain with a view of Honolulu, Pearl Harbor, Hickam Air Force Base and at that time, 1958, a very tiny Honolulu airport. Each floor of the hospital had a large, covered lanai, Hawaiian word for porch, on the ocean side of the building. I spent my afternoons sitting on the third floor lanai looking down on Honolulu and the airport in the distance. I would watch the sun settle into the Pacific Ocean, painting the clouds and city below in tropical shades of pink and orange. There were airplanes taking off into the evening sky, taking people back to distant lands, as other planes landed, bringing tourist to play in the tropical islands. As the darkness gobbled up everything but the city lights below I sat there on the lanai by myself, staring at the distant lights and waited. It was a lonely time.

One day I asked the Nurse Major in charge if I could go get my mail rather than have it delivered to me. It had been about three weeks since my surgery and I thought I was strong enough to manage the long trip to the mail room. I could pick up my own mail and have it a few hours earlier than the delivery to my room. The nurse, a militant Major type barked, "If you're strong enough to pick up your own mail then you're strong enough to go back to your company." When I first landed on her ward I had approached her about helping me become a medical illustrator at the hospital and she was excited by the idea and wanted to help me, but that never happened. After asking her if I could get my own mail I realized that I had ended my own vacation. I would have to go back to my outfit and jump back into training for war.

When I returned to my outfit I was privileged as an artist for I was assigned to straighten out the training aids room. My task was to catalog all of the Army manuals there, hundreds of them. Our company commander, Captain Mortrude, would occasionally ask me to jump in a jeep to go with him to scout a training area. I would draw terrain maps of the area which he would later use for his training sessions. Captain Mortrude was a big, gruff, tough, career Army officer, who made me nervous. I just knew that this soldier, me, was under his thumb. He left the company before I did and before leaving he presented me with a letter of appreciation for my work in his company. "I would be most happy to associate with you again if the opportunity should avail," he added to the end of his letter. I wasn't planning on being in the Army that long.

Sergeant Domai, being convinced that I had bugged out of duty by going on sick call, was extra tough on me when I came back to my outfit. I had to show him the scar from the surgery. I had to do extra pushups. He seemed to have no trouble finding some obscure rule which I had broken and demand that I do extra push-ups to learn my lesson. I would always try to stare at him, maintaining eye contact with him through every push-up as if to say I could take it. He was on me all the time.

Gradually he learned that I wasn't the culprit he initially conceived me to be and we became buddies. We had about as much fun as one could expect training for war at Schofield Barracks. I wonder about Sergeant Domai and the other guys I was with. I wonder if they got gobbled up in the Viet Nam war. The 25th Division at Schofield Barracks was in Hawaii because that was a good jumping off place for far away areas like Viet Nam. The U.S. military involvement there ramped up in the 1960's, long after I was out of uniform, and the

*Private First Class
Lanpher, U.S. Army
Infantry*

conflict continued to 1975. I've read that the 25th Division did go to Viet Nam and was there to protect the western approach to Saigon. I hope they all made it out of that conflict.

For some reason the Army thought I would be good in the weapons platoon as a forward observer for the 81 millimeter mortar squad. When we went out to the field to train, my job would be to direct the mortar squad to fire on a target which only I could see. I would climb up on a hill while the mortar squad would stay far below, behind the hill. I carried a two way radio and binoculars. I would perch myself on top of the hill and pick a target in the distance, a big rock outcropping or a group of bushes. I would estimate the distance and the compass direction to the target and would radio my commands to the mortar squad, "fire when ready". I would sit on the hill and wait for the mortar squad to fire a round over the hill and hopefully over my head to the target in the distance. It would take a couple of attempts to close in on the target, "left one, up two", one round at a time, and then when a round exploded near the target I would radio an adjustment and the final command, "Fire for effect!" On that command the mortar squad would send a group of rounds aimed at their unseen target. Sometimes I could see the rounds high in the sky flying over my head to the target. I was always relieved to see them headed down to the target. It was fun to see the target covered with explosions from the mortar rounds that I had directed. It wasn't drawing for Walt Disney but it did give me an opportunity to study real life effects to store in my mental library, in case I ever got back to the animation business. I later learned that in time of war the forward observer's life expectancy was calculated in minutes. Scary! Today I think they have laser guided things that help the mortar guys to make it all easier. That's what we all need, easier war.

Now that I had my goose egg fixed and knew that I would be in Hawaii for maybe two years, barring a war or something equally disruptive, I began to make plans for my wife to join me. I rented a small, one bedroom, furnished apartment in Waikiki. It was eighty dollars per month and was just steps to the beach. And it was less than two blocks from the Hawaiian Village Hotel and Fort DeRussy on Waikiki Beach. Judy was terrified of flying. Her first flight ever was to join me for a week-long visit at Fort Ord California when I was stationed there. That was a short hop from Burbank and she didn't leave her seat on that flight for fear she would throw the plane off balance. But now she was courageous enough to take the five hour flight to Hawaii by herself. That was about half the time it took me to fly over in the Boeing Stratocruiser. The airlines were now flying their new Boeing 707's so Judy got to fly from Los Angeles to Hawaii in a new jet airliner. She arrived after dark at what was still a tiny Honolulu Airport and we took a taxi to the apartment in Waikiki. We were very excited to be together again so I hurriedly opened the door to our apartment and turned on the lights. I had forgotten to rid the place of uninvited guests. Cockroaches occupied every surface in that apartment. Not the big variety, those came later, these were all of a smaller version. When the light came on it was their cue to end the party and retire into every crack and crevice of that apartment. In a flash they all just disappeared. Judy was terrified of bugs and here we were ready to retire for the evening knowing thousands of bugs were in every crack and cranny in that tiny apartment. Would they come out after we turned off the lights? Would they crawl into bed? Would they walk on our face? It was not an Aloha welcome for Judy or me. She handled it well, though, and was a real pal and companion while we struggled with my military career.

One of my fellow soldiers had been very negative when I had told him my wife was coming to live with me in Waikiki. He had brought his wife over. After she arrived she couldn't find a job, transportation was difficult and they were generally miserable. Judy and I found just the opposite. The first Monday Judy was there she rode the bus to downtown Honolulu to see what job prospects she might find as a bank teller. I couldn't believe she did that. A new big city and she just went for it. She was hired that first day so the bank had a new, young, attractive, bank teller and we had another source of income.

We had a great time riding the bus to the Post Exchange (PX), which was the military grocery store. The prices were very low because the army sold food to us at cost. It was a job benefit. Judy's job helped supplement the one hundred twenty dollars a month the Army paid me as a Private First Class with a wife. I don't ever remember Judy complaining about her job, the bugs, or the low pay I received from the Army or even the one hurricane we experienced there, hurricane Dot it was called. She was kind of excited to have to stuff towels in the un-closable louvered living room windows to keep the rain from blowing in. We survived the hurricane and after awhile the cockroaches were conquered with Residual Raid and a good scrubbing of every surface in that apartment, inside the cabinets and the bottom of the drawers, the bottoms of the sofas and chairs and the under side of the bed. We finally settled into our apartment and on the weekends we would walk over to Waikiki Beach and spend a day loafing like tourists.

Fort DeRussy was a small military base right there on the west end of Waikiki beach. We would have steak dinners at the Fort DeRussy mess hall, a dinner which cost two dollars and ninety five cents each. There was a theater where the admission was twenty five cents. I was a Specialist E4 soldier in the Army when *Sleeping Beauty* was released. My wife and I went to the Fort DeRussy theater to view it and I was thrilled to see my work on the big screen. The movie was placed in the theaters around the country but the box office results were disappointing. It was a visually beautiful film but the audiences didn't take to it.

Judy and I would wake in our tiny little apartment at about four o'clock in the morning, get up and get ready for the day. Judy would fix breakfast, then we would kiss good bye as I stepped out into the dark for the short walk to bus stop. There would always be the trade winds rustling the coconut palms and occasionally I would hear, coming from somewhere in the dark, the hard thump of a large coconut hitting the ground. The hotels removed their coconuts from the trees before they were big enough to cause trouble with someone's head, but some of the private citizens weren't so careful. When I arrived at the Fort DeRussy army bus stop there would already be soldiers waiting, large dark faceless mounds, hunched in the dark on the long benches, waiting for the buses. First come first served. I would usually catch the five o'clock bus to Schofield Barracks, a forty minute ride. I would get there in time to join the ranks of my platoon for revelry at six. When I was unfortunate enough to have KP duty, KP for kitchen police as the kitchen help was called, I would have to report directly to the kitchen. I would be assigned the job of "pots and pans", the least favorite job in the kitchen. The guys that got to the kitchen first, at five in the morning, had their choice of duties, but I was always late because of my morning commute from Waikiki. I would have to wash all of the huge pots and pans that were used for every meal that day. I would work all day in the hot suds, heaving those twenty-quart pots until late in the evening and then with the stench of greasy, sweaty, suds clinging to my every pore I would catch a city bus for the ride back to Waikiki. If I didn't have KP, I would spend the day playing army and training for war until sundown, hoping to catch the last Army bus back to Waikiki for the evening.

Around the beginning of 1959 Judy and I talked about starting a family. We decided the timing would be good because the Army would pay for the hospital care. Judy was pregnant before we finished that conversation. The total hospital bill came to $8.75 and that was for Judy's food. Lisa was born in the evening of November 4th, 1959. That morning, a Wednesday, Judy woke up with labor pains so I called a cab for the long trip from Waikiki, across Honolulu, and up the hills to The Tripler Army Hospital, the same place I'd had my goose egg repaired. A long black limo arrived for our trip,

Tripler Army Hospital, five days after Lisa's birth

apparently an upgrade from the cab company. The limo was driven by a pleasant little old Asian guy and each bump caused my heart to skip a beat, but otherwise we were pretty calm about it. We arrived at the hospital and Judy was admitted to the delivery ward. I bought a Time magazine and settled in the waiting room to wait for Lisa to arrive. That evening, about six o'clock, Lisa decided to be born and it was a glorious event but I don't remember much about it; I was exhausted from waiting all day and I don't remember going back to our apartment in Waikiki. I was a bit numb and very tired because I had attempted to stay awake until Lisa arrived even though I wasn't allowed in the delivery room.

Honolulu Air Terminal, Judy and Lisa ready for the flight home to L.A.

I'm sure Judy felt a lot more worn out than I did for she was the one that had actually given birth. Judy and Lisa stayed at the hospital for about a week and when they were able to leave I went to the hospital in a cab and brought them home.

We had a lot of fun with a new baby in our apartment as well as experiencing all of the angst that new parents suffer. We had no family in Hawaii to support us through those first few weeks but we somehow made it and Lisa survived our parental inexperience. My time in the military was getting short. My outfit was going to the Big Island to play war for thirty days, my second visit there. I would be leaving the Army when I got back to Schofield Barracks. Judy and I decided it would be good if she took the baby Lisa home to California so she wouldn't be alone while I was gone.

Soon it was time to make plans for departing Hawaii. My army tour would be finished in April 1960. Judy made her flight plans, and on the appointed day, the three of us traveled off to the Honolulu airport.

We had hugs and kisses all around and then Judy and Lisa boarded a nice big Boeing 707 and in a few moments they were gone. I vacated our apartment and went back to Schofield Barracks, became a regular soldier again, and took up a bunk in the barracks, alone with about two hundred other guys. Judy and Lisa were going to live with my folks in North Hollywood until I came home. It wasn't an altogether good homecoming for Judy. Two weeks before Judy came home with baby Lisa her parents, who lived in California, decided to move back to Indiana, their original home state. Judy was deeply hurt when she found out they did not care enough to be there when she came home with the baby. It wasn't a very nice thing to do to your daughter, but I guess they thought their reason and time for leaving was important. We had let them borrow our TV while we were in Hawaii, and they took that with them, too. Eventually Judy got to visit Indiana to see her folks, to show off Lisa and brag about her good life, so I guess the pain was eventually diminished. As Oscar Wilde once said, and I do agree, "Living well is the best revenge".

After Judy left I did my thirty days of playing war on the big island of Hawaii. I had experienced being dropped off at an outpost and forgotten while the pretend war raged on in the distant mountains, surviving on only pineapples for food. In the Army I learned that it was important, if possible, to stay dry, warm, clean and organized. If somebody's trying to destroy you it's easier for them if you're wet, cold dirty and hungry.

One night I was sent out to keep watch where there was nothing at all to watch. I was delivered to the middle of the lava fields between Mauna Loa and Muana Kea, the two big volcanoes on the Big Island, as I got out of the jeep the driver said, "Stay here." He meant all night. The lava was nothing but mostly cinders as big as basketballs and bigger, as far as the eye could see. I spent the hours before sundown picking up the smallest pieces of lava I could find. I piled them in a low spot in the big cinders until I had sort of a flat spot to sleep on. It wasn't too cold that night, so when it got dark I took off my field jacket and laid it out on my flat spot as a pretend mattress. There I was, not sure why, to sleep that night in the middle of the lava fields with no other living creature as far as the eye could see, not even a blade of grass for miles in any direction. The next day, a jeep came by to gather me up. I don't remember anyone telling me why I had to do that and I don't remember having a radio, so I couldn't have communicated with anyone had I needed to. At least I wasn't being shot at.

For the rest of those thirty days we played war in the thickest, deepest, dust fields I ever saw. The dust was as fine as dry cake mix and spread like wide rivers between the enormous lava fields. When it was time to go back to Schofield Barracks I was happy to get on the ship back to Oahu. I would spend my last few days at Schofield Barracks clearing post. Clearing post meant checking with all of the post facilities to make sure I didn't owe money or have stuff that didn't belong to me. I was finally transported to Pearl Harbor to board a troop ship for San Francisco.

When I boarded the ship, a Navy troop transport ship, there were dozens, no hundreds, of young Guamanian Navy recruits already on board. They had been picked up in Guam and were all headed to the U.S. for navy boot camp training. The young wannabe sailors occupied most of the bunks and the few soldiers that had boarded the ship were all scrambling for a vacant bunk. I was toting my sixty five pound duffle bag and wasn't in a mood for scrambling for, or sleeping in a bunk with a zillion guys, all packed together. With about three guys to a stack of bunks, and about twelve inches between each guy, it just wasn't the way I wanted to sleep. There wasn't much room for breathing, and besides there wasn't any fresh air to breathe. I milled about with a couple other guys until all the bunks were taken. An officer appeared and announced that those of us without bunks were to follow him. He led us to a forward part of the ship, up near the bow, where there were dozens of bunks which seemed much cleaner, nicer and newer than the ones in the aft part of the ship. I picked a bunk away from the other guys and felt like I had won the lottery. I had at least five days and nights to spend on this ship so at least I would have a fairly comfortable place to sleep.

Each morning, just after sun up, we would have to report to the stern for a reading of the duty roster. The stern of the ship was where most of the guys hung out all day. They would lay around with the smoke from the ship's stacks billowing down around them. Half the time there was black soot fluttering about like wind blown snow. I had found a passage to the forward deck, under the bridge, where I spent my days after the duty roster was read. I would lay in the sunshine, shirt off and pants rolled up, below the bridge of the ship, as the clean, fresh, Pacific Ocean breezes would fill the sails of my dreams, dreams of being out of the Army and back with my wife and daughter and working at Disney's on animated films. It was about the second morning out to sea when everyone was gathered at the stern to hear the officer in charge read the alphabetized duty roster. There would be several guys picked each morning to do the necessary chores to keep the ship maintained. As the officer called off the names and the guys whose names were called would answer, he called out a name that was just before mine. The guy didn't answer. Again the name was read, again no answer, and a question was yelled out, "Any one seen Landis." No answer. When the officer looked back down at his duty roster he started with the name after mine, "Larson." Larson yelled "Yo" and at that moment I knew I would spend the rest of my voyage in the clean fresh ocean air of the forward deck. The officer had skipped my name!

Five days later as our ship was approaching San Francisco Bay on a very foggy morning we were met by a flotilla of small fishing vessels all headed out to sea, hundreds of them, sailing in the opposite direction. I don't know how we kept from hitting one, the glory of radar I guess, and a lone sailor on the bow with binoculars, staring into the wall of solid fog. Five days at sea, on a

Navy ship, full of excited young guys from Guam coming to America to be trained for a hitch in the U.S. Navy and I was excited because I was going to be discharged from the Army. I was on the forward deck and elated to see the Golden Gate Bridge swelling up out of the fog to greet us. We sailed under it into San Francisco Bay and on to the Oakland Terminal.

After spending two weeks at an Army clearing depot in Oakland, making sure my records were clean, I finally flew home. Judy picked me up at the Lockheed-Burbank Air Terminal and we were very happy to see each other, young and in love is so splendid and we were that. We drove to my parent's house in North Hollywood where Judy had been living. I was so excited about being released from the military that I forgot I was the father of a baby girl. Lisa was asleep in her crib in the bedroom and after all the hugs and kisses from Mom and Dad my mother said, "Aren't you forgetting someone?" I raced into the bedroom to see my new daughter sleeping peacefully in her crib, totally oblivious to her father's excitement. The family was all together again.

It was time to find an apartment for the three of us and for me to get back to my career at Disney, a career that had been put on hold by none other than the President of the United States of America. I survived the Army and by being in the Army during a slump at Disney's animation, I survived a layoff. I was back to work by April 1960, ready to resume my position at Walt Disney Productions, a much wiser and more grateful twenty five year old.

CHAPTER 5
A short stop at DisNey

I was relieved and grateful to be back at the studio and very excited to be assigned as Dan McManus's assistant on *101 Dalmatians*. Dan was an old-timer and had been a prominent fixture in the effects department since the 1930's. He lived in a very nice home in Toluca Lake, a neighborhood for many of the movie stars of the thirties and forties, the likes of Bing Crosby and Bob Hope. Dan lived there with his much younger wife and her two young children from an earlier marriage. He was of the old school. He had a horse stabled over at Griffith Park and wore his fancy riding clothes to work on the days he planned to ride. He had a gold pocket watch with a gold chain hanging from the watch pocket in his vest. He would, on occasion, theatrically pull out his pocket watch to check the time, illustrating in one swoop that he was a man of distinction who knew what time it was. He was born in Mexico but had been brought to the United States as an infant. He still managed to keep his accent sounding just enough like Ricardo Montalban to appear as a worldly person of culture.

Dan and I had rooms at the end of the A wing of the animation building, the first wing at the entrance to the animation building. My room was just outside his and from either of our rooms we could look out on the street which was the walk way for all of the girls who worked in the Ink and Paint Department. Dan's Occasional announcement to "Up periscope" would alert me to look out my window as there'd be a pretty girl or two walking by outside. My youthful, twenty-five years of age, led me to believe Dan was a spry old guy for sixty years old but he did sometimes need his naps. I would come back from lunch and he would be asleep in his KEM Weber designed lounge chair. With my work ethic in overdrive I would nervously wonder if I should wake him or let him run his own naps. I was his animation assistant and he was the boss so I would let him nap.

Dan was generous to work with and gave me the task of animating the effects on a few scenes as well as all of the assistant work on his animation. During the period I was working with him he was asked to do some freelance effects animation on a Ray Harryhausen film, *Jason and the Argonauts*. He asked me to do his assistant work on the project and I was more than happy help. Years later I had an opportunity to meet Mr. Harryhausen and to thank him for all of the great film work that he had done. He was a very pleasant man and pleased and humbled that I should express my appreciation for his efforts.

When I came back to work for Disney I was told that the studio was required to hire me back in the same position I had when I was drafted. I think the studio had to keep me in that position for three months. After the three months I was demoted, with a pay cut, to "break-down artist", a classification below assistant. As it turned out, it was another flyin' chunk to duck. Dan had a previous assistant who had retired and realized he couldn't afford retirement so he ask if he could come back to work at the studio as Dan's assistant. Since the old guy had appealed to someone's heart he got my job. Or maybe he was a more talented effects artist. Ouch!

I was then assigned to Cliff Nordberg, a very talented character animator. I worked under Bud Hester, Cliff's assistant. Much later Bud left Disney's animation department and became the Screen Cartoonist Union Business Representative, a position he held until he retired. Cliff, having started at the studio in the early forties, was a character animator on many of the Disney movies. When I started working with Cliff he was just beginning animation on the first Disney color television show *The Wonderful World of Color* starring Professor Ludwig Von Drake, a wacky, older, more educated relative of Donald Duck. It was my first official position in the character department. Cliff was a good mentor and allowed me to do some of the assistant work which would normally have gone to his assistant Bud. I never heard Bud complain so it must have been okay. Cliff was a very talented, energetic, interesting, curious guy, and we had some fun discussions about life and flyin' chunks to duck. In fact I still have a book he gave me, *Speak for Yourself* by Jessica Somers Driver. He especially liked the third chapter which spoke of a "listening attitude". Somers said that listening puts one in a state of positive expectancy and focuses thought outward. So my working with the great talented mentors at the studio was more than learning the art of animation, it was also rounding out my life philosophy and helping me to construct survival modes.

Eager for success, I was jumping at every chance to do freelance. I would take work home from the studio, Donald Duck scenes, anything that required follow-up drawings needed to complete the animation. I would earn seven dollars a film foot, which was sixteen frames on thirty-five millimeter film. Sometimes there would be three or four drawings which I would need to do, or maybe six or seven drawings, depending on how many key drawings had already been done in that film foot. I had to draw fast to make any money. Business meets Art. I had an animation desk in the living room of the apartment and I would work long hours into the night. One of the assistant animators, a strong union man who I was working with objected to me taking freelance work home because he felt it would diminish the number of jobs for full time artists. One day he came driving into the studio in a nice little sports car he had just purchased. The funds used to purchase that car was reported, allegedly, or so I heard, or someone said, to have come from work which he took home and completed. Not only the drawings an assistant should do but all of the drawings in the scene, drawings that could have been done by the follow up artists in the studio, which would have included me. I feel ashamed for having believed that story. Beware the too self righteous person for their eyes may be peering into yours while their hand is in your pocket.

One day I received a phone call from an effects artist named Fred Miller who had quit Disney and was working for a little studio in Santa Monica called Technical Communications Incorporated, or TCI. They needed an effects animator, artist, and illustrator, all in one. Fred and I had become friends when he was working at Disney's and he was offering me the job. We liked guitars and he had accompanied me as we visited many pawn shops around Los Angeles looking for a nice classical guitar. We found a nice classical, acoustic, Giannini for $40. It was my first guitar, made in Brazil with Brazilian rosewood and a very tight spruce top. Before buying it I got permission from the pawn shop owner to take the guitar to the Giannini distributor in Los Angeles. The distributor man said it was a beautiful guitar and well worth the price which should have been a couple hundred dollars. I bought the guitar and was so thrilled with it that I proceeded to write a letter to the Giannini people in Sao Paula Brazil, giving them the make and model numbers of my trophy guitar. I received a letter from the president of the Company who told me the guitar was made in Brazil but he was happy that I had it and that I was interested in its history. Fine guitars are made with glues and materials which are appropriate for their given climates. My guitar was made for Brazil but someone from Brazil had brought my guitar to L.A. and, I would guess, had to hock it at a pawn shop for money to live on. Their misfortune allowed me to give their beautiful guitar a great, fun-filled, loving home. The dry climate of California apparently had no effect on my guitars construction and it held up well. The generous Giannini Company sent me a monthly guitar magazine for several years after that. Unfortunately I could never read one for they were always written in Portuguese.

Judy and I were living with our baby in Sun Valley, just northeast of North Hollywood. We had bought a house which was seriously in need of paint and repairs, mostly cosmetic. We spent a year washing, scraping, painting, pounding, carpeting, fixing and replacing stuff until our house became a comfortable home. It was on a corner lot in Sun Valley and we paid $12,950 for it. Just down the street from us there lived an accountant who worked at the studio. He had said he earned $150 a week at the studio. I thought $150 a week would be all I would need. Ever! I had begun to have altruistic thoughts of responsibility to the world, some sort of a need to do something I thought more important than cartoons. Working on animated cartoons didn't seem to be it, maybe working on films teaching stuff, technical films explaining how things work, maybe for the aerospace industry. Maybe that would be more important than cartoons. Looking back I think it was just a desire for more success, measured by the number of people who wanted to use my talent, and how much they were willing to pay me for it. It was 1962 when Fred made me the offer to come to work at TCI. The offer was $100 a week with a ten per cent raise in one year. I would animate effects and do art work on technical films. Rocket launches, satellites in space, submarines under water, nuclear blasts, all fun stuff. The pay wasn't much more than I was earning at Disney but it was a bit of a raise and a chance to do more art and animation. I handed in the customary letter of resignation at Disney and took the job with Fred. It wasn't the $150 a week, but Disney had cut my pay and these people were going to pay me a bit more with a raise in one year and the small company looked as if it would grow.

The films we worked on were technical films designed to teach people how these things worked. How they were built, and how the weapons of war were advancing. I painted backgrounds, airbrushed renderings, and animated stuff. I worked cheap, and even helped out on the animation camera and live action shoots. The building we worked in was a bit of a drive for me. It was on little Santa Monica Boulevard just west of Century City. It was a nice two story building so the studio was up off the street with a big window that looked out on the bustle of the Boulevard. While working there I won an award from the Industrial Film Producers Association for layout and animation on a film called *The Persuasive Push*, with the subtle of *ION propulsion in space*. It was a busy year but at the end of that year instead of a raise I received a thank you and good bye. I was laid off. Fred wasn't much fun anymore. Over time I lost touch with Fred and sadly, he died a few years later.

I applied for and got my job back at the "mouse house". I was back with Cliff Nordberg who was now starting work on the feature film, *The Sword and the Stone,* the story of King Arthur as a boy. Cliff was animating the character Wart and he again let me do assistant work on some of his scenes. He was a very easy and helpful mentor and helped me greatly to add to my animation knowledge. I still wanted more stuff and even though life was good, I was open to opportunity. Nearing the end of that production I received a call from Bob Hyskell. Bob had been a fellow effects artist but left the studio for a position with Lytle Corporation, down off Washington Boulevard by the ocean, near Venice. He said he needed help on a film project. The company had a contract with the Navy and I would be doing art and animation for technical films. Bob said he could offer me three months work at one hundred fifty dollars a week, nonunion. Wow. But I couldn't leave the security of Disney's for a promise of three months of nonunion work. I had a wife, a daughter, a dog, a car and a house, and a lawn. I was now a twenty-seven year old man of responsibility. Several weeks later Bob called and said it looked more like a six-month project. After thinking about it for about two minutes I took the job. Again resigning from Disney's, I went to work for The Lytle Corporation. Bob and two other artists worked in the film unit. Earlier, John Mildenberger had quit Disney to work there. I barely knew John at Disney's but now that there were only four of us working together we developed a working friendship. The forth artist was a gentleman named Lyn Gray; Bob had hired him some time before.

It turned out that Lytle Corporation was at one time a huge company doing technical films and manuals for large defense contractors all over the country, but now the company was in its last struggles with corporate death, having suffered what seemed to be a typically natural, corporate evolution of birth, life, and death. It seems companies become successful because of the inspiration and very hard work of a few. To make it easier on people, assistants are hired for the managers, then secretaries for the assistants. Then the new vice president's assistants need secretaries. Next a human resources department is needed because there are so many people problems, and on and on until the bureaucratic bloat gets in the way of business. The arteries harden and the heart struggles to pump life through all the bureaucratic clots. The guys who started it all are fat and want to kick back with golden parachutes and who can blame them. So the corporation sputters without the original inspiration and eventually goes bankrupt. Not all companies follow this trajectory. The Walt Disney Company has been up and down, but mostly up; The company changes and grows and struggles but never dies, the trend has always been up. But I had left Disney's for a company whose trend line was definitely going down fast, not smart. I should have learned about trend lines before leaving Disney's.

The four of us were the only people working in one room of a large building. Across the hall was a big room filled with office furniture and typewriters, the new IBM roller-ball typewriters, no computers then, trash receptacles, chairs, staplers, and more. I still have my stapler. That room was the corporate graveyard. The rest of the building was ominously empty. We had fun working there for there was very little outside interference. Occasionally some Navy guys would visit for a look at what we were doing. We did some animated films about submarines and sidewinder missiles. We did some slide films on Vietnamese characters, top-secret stuff. Didn't know at the time that there would later be a nasty war in Viet Nam and the characters we researched would be at the heart of it. Eventually we finished the Navy work and the result was we had worked ourselves out of a job. Well, not quite.

While we were finishing up our work, a company called EMC Corporation in Minneapolis, Minnesota, took an interest in us as a film unit. They were in the educational materials business and wanted a film unit to do educational films. They had purchased one of the most prominent Hollywood sound studios, Universal Radio Recorders, and we were now owned by them as a division called Film Designers. The main offices of Universal Radio Recorders were down on Santa Monica Boulevard just west of Highland Avenue but they put us in one of their buildings on Sunset Boulevard at Highland Avenue, across the corner from Hollywood High School. We all remember where we were when President Kennedy got shot, and that's where I was, working in that tiny studio on Highland Avenue, November 22, 1963.

The building was a recording studio and our little downstairs offices were just a part of it. The upstairs sound studios had been frequented by many famous entertainers including the man himself, Frank Sinatra. The company thought we were important enough to have a secretary. Her desk was to be in the very small lobby where the floor had a slope which made sitting at the desk a bit of a struggle. On her first day of work our new secretary arrived early to make a good impression and everything began professionally, but later in the morning the quiet was shattered by a clattering sound. I looked around to see the poor girl falling backward in her chair, sliding down that sloping floor. I jumped up to help but by the time I got to her, she and her chair, with the wheels still spinning, were both upside down, sliding to a stop. As I helped her up I felt much empathy for her but the words that came out of my mouth didn't convey that very well, "Gee, and on your first day, too!" She brushed herself off, grabbed her purse, and left. She never came back. Nobody remembers the second guy to fly solo across the Atlantic and I don't remember our next secretary. I guess she didn't do anything as noteworthy as our first secretary.

Universal Radio Recorders had been, for years, a big name in the recording business. It seems all of the big name entertainers dropped by to do commercial bits or music. Frank Sinatra with Billie May recorded upstairs one evening. Elvis did an album at the Santa Monica studios. Mickey Rooney, Phyllis Diller, George Gobel, Barbara Eden, Jack Benny, I got to meet a bunch of famous folks but I never had the opportunity to meet Frank or Elvis. But I did get to stand next to Jack Benny as we both visited the men's room. It was an important studio.

We puttered along in our tiny little studio, doing animation for Navy films and some film strip illustrations, all fun artwork. This was the early sixties. Feeling important and trying to look business- like, I wore a jacket and a neck tie to work. These were the hippie days and Hollywood was teaming with them. The hippies that were living in that neighborhood would occasionally harass me, making fun of my dressed up look, as I walked from my car to the studio. Of course they were opposed to the establishment because to be established you have to work and they were mostly opposed to work. The hippies apparently discovered that the commune style of living allowed the people to be free, free from work. Those who didn't like to work could be taken care of by people who knew there was work to be done if one is to eat and stay clean. So the worlds many commune experiments have failed for there always seems to be more people who want their needs met by others than people who want to meet other people's needs, other than their own. There are still hippie communes around but now we call them homeless shelters.

We were doing some work for the Navy, mostly the U.S Navy Ordinance Test Station, or NOTS, whose main headquarters was in the Mojave Desert with an annex in Pasadena. We continued to work for the Navy and made some other contacts as well. There was an important film for the Navy that explained a new more powerful electric motor so I learned about electric motors. And I learned about Navy secrecy. The Navy needed some films to teach submariners about their nuclear submarines so I learned about nuclear sub construction and stern plain jams. I learned that I could never work in a submarine. We connected with some young computer experts with the idea to make a series of ten-minute films teaching computer programming. This was long before anyone had done any worthwhile animation with the computer. So I learned a little about computer programming and this was just the beginning of computers. I got to go with a live action film crew down to the North American Aviation plant to film the new, full sized, scale model of the B1 bomber that North American was going to build for the military. I got to help light the interior of a very crowded cabin so the windows of the exterior shots wouldn't look like black holes. So I learned about jet bombers, inside and out and I learned that those hot lights could set those plastic seats on fire. But if you move the lights away real quick and rub down the hot bubbling plastic no one will notice that you didn't set the very expensive, multi million dollar full sized, model, on fire while all of those people watched with camera's rolling.

Later, there was space made available for us in the building on Santa Monica Boulevard, so we moved over there. There was a Shakey's Pizza right across the street and not as many hippies. We had an agent and more space. We eventually developed some films for both the Southern Baptist Missouri Synod and Lutheran Television. For the Baptist we did a series of short children's films using a character named Jot. Jot would get into situations that allowed the story to serve up some religious lesson. Our relationship with Lutheran Television produced three one-half hour television shows that would be given to the television networks to promote the Lutheran message. For the first show my title of *Christmas Is* was accepted by the other guys and the second I called *Easter Is*. Another was called *The City That forgot About Christmas.* We did an animated film for the American Cancer society called *The Three Faces of Stanley.* The title was a take on the movie *The Three Faces of Eve.* The society had a live action version but they found that motion pictures showing advancing colon cancer didn't appeal to the rubber chicken lunch crowd. One day Bob Hyskell and I went down to L.A. for a meeting of the American Cancer Society with about fifteen of their executives. As we sat around a big table discussing the film the question came up about a finish date for the film. Bob without a blink, or without having discussed any of this with me turned to me and said "Dorse will talk to you about that", Uh no, no time to duck the chunks. I never forgave him for putting me on the spot. He was the one that was in charge of the schedule and should have answered the question. I must have been brilliant at dancing around an answer for a gentleman came up to me after the meeting and said "You're very fast on your feet." I'm not sure that was complimentary.

Bob is dead now. After couple of heart surgeries, for which a few of us donated blood, he eventually began to smoke again and drink a lot of Jim Beam. Just like the old days when he and I partied into the night in Fort Worth, Texas, after those long exhausting days we would have while meeting with the Lutheran Television people. Well, Jim Beam and smoking cigarettes and that was that. Bob was always a nervous guy.

CHAPTER 6

Broken Brain, Marriage Malfunction, and Career collapse

It began in the early 1960's; I guess the work stress started to conflict with my Buddha nature. I began to have anxiety attacks which confused and scared me. Simple tasks were becoming very difficult. Just waiting at the McDonald's window to order some fun food for my daughter and I would become an anxiety producing event. A shopping mall would become, for me, a scary prison and being there would fill me with fear. I just wanted nothing more than to extricate myself from the confines of the mall to rid me of the emotional impact that the fear was causing.

During these troubling times I would push myself. I would go to a mall or place myself in a situation which had previously caused anxiety to see if I could overcome whatever it was that had its hold on me. No matter how much I pushed the fear, the anxiety pushed back and became even more frightening. I began to have thoughts of self destruction and scarier yet, the destruction of others. Even now this sounds hard for me to believe but at the time even sitting down to dinner became a test of my control. I developed a strange fear of sharp things, which of course made me even more distrusting of myself. My drive home from work would be a test of endurance. Attempting to make it home before I became unglued created a vague fear of just losing control. Oddly enough, at the time I didn't have problems continuing with my work where I had a structured environment even though at times it was very difficult to make that drive to work. My dilemma was becoming more puzzling for me each day.

Confiding in Judy prompted her to call a psychiatrist who told her in rather "another wife pissed at her husband mode" that I would have to make the call myself if there was a problem. I went to a doctor who gave me a vitamin B-12 shot which is supposed to have a calming effect but what I needed was a head transplant. By this time I was giving much thought to my mental and emotional state because I felt that my spiral of insanity could only have an end which would result in my total demise. That was unless I, me, my mind, my thoughts, where ever, what ever place reason existed in me could stop the spiral and let the reason prevail. I realized that whatever thoughts my brain was producing were thoughts alien to what I wanted for myself. One night I got out of bed to go to the bathroom and as I walked toward the bathroom it occurred to me that I felt great, it was just a moment but I felt normal, stress free and I realized for that moment I wasn't thinking, I was free from thought! Those days my brain seemed to have its own agenda for its thoughts. Many of those thoughts were alien and frightening so I made an agreement with my brain. I gave my brain permission to think what ever thoughts it could conjure up no matter how scary. "Brain," I said, "you just go to town and have all the horror thoughts you want." I made a declaration that I would not act on them. I had been reading, searching for answers, in many books of philosophy and reason.

One day I found a quote in a magazine article by a Greek philosopher by the name of Epictetus. His thought helped me to begin an end to my downward mental spiral. Epictetus was born a Grecian slave in 55 B.C. and eventually became a philosopher with his own school where he taught the stoicism school of philosophy founded upon the teachings of Zeno of Citium. Citium was a Greek colony and Zeno was born there and lived from 333 B.C. to 264 B.C. Of the many thoughts that Epictetus noted, the one that helped me to see things differently was this; "Man is disturbed not by things but by the view he takes of those things." An easy example in today's world would be an automobile with a number of occupants which has the misfortune to hit and kill a dog. All of the people in the car will have a different view of the same occurrence. The little lady that owns a poodle may become hysterical. The man who comes from a culture that eats dogs may be upset because he is reminded of dinner and his trip is delayed, caring little about the dog except as wasted food. If there is a veterinarian in the car he may be very adult and make an attempt to save the animal, and so it goes, everyone with a differing view of the same event. A view that disturbs some and not others only because of the way they choose to think of what has happened.

Epictetus put my thinking on a new track which seemed very reasonable to me. I was in need of changing my view of how I fit into the world. Too bad those Greek philosophers have been minimized in our culture. It was a couple thousand years ago that those philosophers were so brilliant with their positive ideas about successfully living life. Still today many people of the world are clamoring about, pushing their unreasonable beliefs on others, sometimes to the point of violence. And many of the world's naive suffer continued painful indignities, even death, while the loud voices of unreason drown out those voices of the ancient philosophers.

Another experience which helped to solidify this idea of Epictetus was a time with my daughter at a public playground where she was playing in a very large sand filled area. Around the perimeter of the sand box was a concrete curb about six inches high and four inches wide. As my daughter enjoyed her play time in the sand I was casually balancing on the curb and walking around the sand box. It occurred to me that if that curb was forty or fifty feet in the air or even twenty feet off the ground I would have great difficulty staying balanced on that curb as I walked. Balancing is the act of correcting on negative feedback just as a missile does when seeking its target. I realized that if I were twenty feet in the air on that narrow curb my safety would be altered because my nervous sense of danger would counter my negative feed back. I balanced fine at six inches but just thinking that I was twenty feet in the air made me less stable.

All of my mental strain seemed diminished when I had work to do at the studio. At Film Designers we made an effort to get a TV cartoon series going by developing a pilot film for an animated series I called *Fabulous Fables,* which was to be about animals. The pilot was a story about tigers and why all the other cats climb trees but the tigers don't. So I learned a little bit about tigers. And I learned about having to fire people when one of my animators decided he was going to tell me how to direct the film. He went to my boss to convince him that I needed to be fired but my boss fired him. He had consistently animated scenes that were contradictory to my direction and was costing us money because of it. So he was fired. He later got into some serious trouble with The Walt Disney Company so I guess I pegged his character correctly.

By now the *Fabulous Fables* pilot had used up all our profits and since a network didn't pick it up we were sort of out of business. Most definitely out of business when our parent company, in May, 1971, said "You guys are fired." So I learned about being fired.

Losing my job at this time wasn't very helpful because my marriage to Judy was going through some growing pains. Pains caused by us mostly growing apart. We had sold our house in Sun Valley, thinking we had made a killing, and had bought a house in Canoga Park. It was a nice house with a grammar school which Lisa attended on the next street over. Judy, not one for participating in the neighborhood coffee klatches would have her household chores done by mid morning and had become very bored as a stay at home mom. I was working hard at that time, driving from Canoga Park to Hollywood every day on the Ventura Freeway with all of the traffic and meeting some atrocious deadlines for the films we were doing. I was also trying to recover from the ghastly experience of suffering though what I think was a nervous breakdown while trying to present a sane person to the outside world. I was beginning to be a more comfortable me, a new me, a born again Dorse, my own person with a view of the world which was starting to work for me.

With my new-found thoughts about how to recover from my hellish world I gradually started to feel better. Judy would react to this as if I was having too much fun out in the world all day leaving her home alone. She was becoming more lonely and bored as I was becoming more confident with the new me. She would try to fill her days by making huge paper flower arrangements or bowls and bowls of big acrylic grapes. The impatience with her life was being reflected on me and she would want me to walk in the house and sit down to the dinner she had prepared so she could clean up the kitchen and relax for the evening. Judy decided that she needed more life in her life so she started school to study for a real estate license. That was the beginning of a very different dynamic in our family structure. Judy got her real estate license. Why, I don't know, but we decided to sell our house in Canoga Park. We put it on the market and it sold before we found another that we liked so we moved into an apartment on Canoga Avenue in Woodland Hills, just a few doors up from Ventura Boulevard. Lisa started the seventh grade of junior high school while we were living there. Judy spent a lot of weekends working, oh those real estate hours. Lisa and I spent a lot of weekend time together, without Judy.

Judy and I became more difficult with each other. There were loud arguments and much banging around. We had come to a point where there was zero intelligent discussion. We each would just react to the other's insanity. During one of these altercations, out of angry desperation, and to frighten her into some sort of quiet I grabbed my guitar and smashed it into tiny pieces. So much for giving my guitar a great, fun-filled, loving home, I still hate myself for that outburst, maybe hate is too strong. It was just a really stupid thing to do. I loved my Giannini. I had bought a guitar case and lined it with pieces of an old fur coat I had purchased at a thrift shop. It was beautiful. My guitar fit in the case perfectly, snugly, lovingly. For years I kept the pieces of the Gianinni in a brown paper bag and stored the case in the closet as some sort of symbol for some sort of something. There is just no making sense of insanity.

Judy and I eventually ended up getting a divorce. Everybody gets hurt, children, girlfriends, wives, husbands, all. Judy didn't protest or contest the divorce. She kept her new white 1972 leather lined Cadillac, which she had purchased with cash, to aid in her real estate sales. A Ford just wouldn't do. I gave her the furniture. I kept my 1968 Pontiac Firebird which I loved more than anything else but she didn't like it for I could drive it very fast. I moved into the Lakeside Apartments in Burbank and began a single life. That wasn't easy for anybody but no doubt it was toughest on Lisa for her parents had become irresponsible, self-centered, imbeciles. I'm sure it left scars on the three of us. The divorce was final in October, 1974. I remember going to the grocery store and actually wondering what I needed to buy just to live. Food? Windex? Ajax? Coffee? Paper towels and toilet paper? What? A few years later Burt Reynolds starred in a movie entitled *Starting Over*. It was like the story of my life.

This was the early seventies, time was flying and I was out of my marriage and out of work. Oh what to do? Well, there were five of us now that had worked for Film Designers and we were all out of work so we all voted to form a partnership. I quickly discovered that a partnership with five partners is like being married to four spouses. All of us were artists with artist's temperaments and very little business savvy. We called our partnership Image Arts and continued to do film work for the Navy. We made some other contacts as well but it was a struggle. We did some technical films for the Navy Weapons Lab at China Lake California, a Navy installation out in the Mojave Desert. We would do the artwork, explaining how some new scary bomb worked and then I would take the art out to the desert to show the Naval officers in charge of the project how the animation worked. I would have to leave in the morning before the sun came up and I wouldn't get home until the sun was down. Actually the toughest part of the day would be trying to keep the Navy guys from ruining my artwork by poking it with their pens to show me something that would let me know how smart they were.

But our Image Arts business partnership was failing and the Navy work dwindled to nothing. There was a period when I finally had to file for unemployment. It was very depressing, standing in line at the employment office in Hollywood with dozens of out of work, want to be actors. It was so depressing I went back to work. I found some freelance to do. I had come to a turning point. I knew I must point my career in another direction. I informed my partners that my share of Image Arts was for sale and the share was quickly snapped up. My share was worth $600, seriously.

CHAPTER 7

The Rescuers Rescue Me

Severly in need of employment, I secured an appointment for an interview at, you guessed it, Walt Disney Productions. It was early 1975. I had been absent from the studio for over ten years so I didn't know what to expect. Walt had died in 1966, during my absence, so the studio could be an entirely different place for me, but I wanted a job as an effects animator so I would have to face the music. I was asked to bring a portfolio to the meeting. Along with my art portfolio I had a short 15 minute film, *Uncle Tom and His Magic Tree.* I had directed the animation and did some of the animating along with my partners. It was done for the Southern Council of Optometrists and was a pretty nice little film.

The day of my interview I met with Jack Buckley, Ed Hansen, and Don Duckwall. The animation department heads decided that they would hire me but as an assistant animator. I thought my stuff was animator material but I guess they thought I needed to be humbled. I was hired as an assistant animator for Jack Buckley who was working on *The Rescuers* and was now the effects department supervisor. Thanks to Jack, six months later I was promoted to animator. I was enjoying my work on that film directed by John Lounsbery and Wolfgang Reitherman, two of the Nine Old Men. Around the studio Wolfgang was known as Woolie. He had started at Disney in 1933 and left to join the Army Air Corps in WWII. He became an ace pilot before returning to the studio. I didn't work with John Lounsbery on *The Rescuers,* I worked with Woolie, he was intimidating but he seemed to like my work and was always very professional and likable.

One day Jack assigned a scene to me that was only five feet long: a short but complex scene where the paddle steamer is sinking in the swamp. The alligators have been trapped in the elevator cage of the paddle steamer as the fireworks are lighting up the sky. The old boat explodes in a ball of flame as the elevator cage and the alligators are blown sky high. As the boat's smoke stacks flail about, debris is blown into the air and rains down around the boat and splashes into the swamp. It wasn't a character scene with the importance of one of the film's stars, but it was going to be fun. I set to work and decided I would do a pose test, rendering the drawings with pastels so the test could be shot in color. To shoot a pose test in color was against the rules but I thought this scene needed to be storyboarded and presented in all its blazing color. I finally finished the renderings of each pose and sent my scene to camera. In those non-digital days we would have to wait three or four days for our film to come back from processing before we would know whether we had a hit or a miss. I busied myself with other work while waiting for my scene to come back from the camera department.

Joe Morris, an administrative assistant and a lovable fixture at the studio, delivered the film to us from the film lab. I was always excited to see if a scene was working when I viewed the film so I thanked Joe, closed the door to my room to insure that my first viewing would be a private affair and excitedly threaded the Moviola, a small film viewing machine. I carefully pressed the slow peddle to make sure the film was threaded properly and then moved my foot over to the peddle which would send the film through the Moviola at ninety feet per minute, a speed which could chew up the best of scenes if the film was not properly threaded on the sprockets. The frames of my pose test flew by, projected on the little Moviola screen, and I liked what I saw. I decided to show the scene to Jack. He didn't make a fuss about the test being in color, he liked what he saw. Sometimes he would show our scenes to Woolie without the animators present, but this time he said "Let's show it to Woolie." Gulp!

My scene was cut into a reel with other scenes that needed to be shown to Woolie that day. Jack and I, with our reel of film, headed up to the second floor offices of the director, Wolfgang Reitherman. I got the job of threading the film in the Moviola as Jack chatted with Woolie. I didn't have a chance to try the slow pedal which I would usually do to make sure the Moviola was threaded properly but Woolie was ready for the show. Waving his cigar in the air, (we could still smoke in the studio in those days and many people did) he sat down in a chair and rolled up to the Moviola as Jack and I gathered around behind him. Being the straight-forward, no holds barred kind of guy that he was, he slammed his foot down on the fast pedal and away we went. I was relieved that the film was threaded properly and the film was flying through the machine at twenty four frames a second without being shredded.

As the black and white pencil test scenes whizzed by Woolie intently studied them, without comment, as Jack and I watched over his shoulder.

Suddenly the tiny Moviola screen exploded with color as my short posed test flashed by in about three point three seconds. Woolie threw up his hand holding his cigar and reared back with a loud, "Whoa!" Taking his foot off the pedal, the machine stopped. He slowly turned, waving his cigar in the air, craning his neck around so he could look me in the eye, and as a master of timing he paused for an intimidating moment as our eyes united. Just before the silence became fatal for me he said with confident emphasis, "You'll never get that in final." I choked on the challenge ready to quote *The Little Engine That Could*, "I think I can, I think I can," but Woolie didn't need to hear it. Without giving me a chance to comment he turned back to the Moviola to view the rest of the pencil tests. Of course my brain was whirling with wonder at what Woolie meant by his terse statement. I had other moments with Woolie but that one made me wonder if Woolie's response was a way to get the best out of people. Maybe he liked my rough pose test and wanted to make sure that I would succeed with the final scene and fear would motivate me to do that. Woolie had so much studio history behind him, so many years of experience in animation; it was a serious jolt to my ego to hear him say, "You'll never get that in final."

With Woolie's words ringing in my ears I set to work hoping to prove him wrong. After animating all of the scene's elements on paper, the ship's smoke stacks, the flying debris, the fireworks, the water rippling, the fireball, I sent the scene out for a pencil test, the pencil drawings shot on black and white film. While waiting for the test to come back from camera, I confidently rendered my animated fireball drawings on paper with Prisma color pencils, cut them out and glued them on cels for the final color take. (The word cel is what animators call a sheet of transparent celluloid used in the animation art process.) Woolie approved the pencil test so I sent the scene out, all of the drawings along with my rendered fireball drawings glued to the cels. It was all to be put through the system, animation checking, ink and paint, final checking, camera, and finally the film would end up in the final color reel. Woolie approved the final color take without ceremony and I was happy and relieved. That scene was just a very, very, tiny part of the many successful Walt Disney animated films but the memory of Woolie waving his cigar about still hangs in my head.

I remember the last scene I animated on *The Rescuers*. It was the scene at the end of the film where Madame Medusa was in the river riding the alligators. I had animated the water and the river boat smoke stacks as Medusa smacks into them with a splatter of soot. I finished my last drawing at about five o'clock and went upstairs to the Penthouse Club to join the group at a small wrap party, a very small party compared to what the gigantic parties would become in the future.

The Penthouse Club was on the top floor of the animation building; there was a bar and restaurant, a barbershop and a gym. It was an all male club, a remnant of Walt's good old boy's early days. To join, one had to be at a certain level of employment, male, and be sponsored by a member of the club. In the 1970's the club was shut down by Ron Miller, then President, when a few of the ladies in the studio protested an all male club. Rather than admit women to an all male club Ron's solution was to turn the place into a nice restaurant for managers and people who were close enough to managers to be invited to dine there. When we finished *The Rescuers* in 1977, Jack Buckley decided to retire and I was bumped up to supervisor of special effects. *The Rescuers* reported budget was under $2 million and the domestic gross was just under $50 million. Not a blockbuster but I think the studio was happy and I was happy to have been a part of it.

While we were finishing *The Rescuers* the studio was beginning the production of a live action/animation musical romp called *Pete's Dragon* starring Helen Reddy, Jim Dale, Mickey Rooney and Red Buttons. After my work on *The Rescuers* our special effects department was assigned the hand drawn effects which helped to bring the dragon to life. Don Bluth, one of the promising stars of the animation department was directing the animation. My work on this picture was noted in the book, *Disney A to Z,* first published by Hyperion in 1996. The book was put together by Dave Smith, the man who began the Walt Disney Archives in 1970 and has been the director since its beginning.

On the back lot where *The Absent Minded Professor* was shot there was movie set. It was a lovely Middle American neighborhood with curving streets and those Victorian styled homes. Some of our artists discovered that one of the houses had a swimming pool so occasionally some of our more adventuresome artists, working on the weekend, would take a break from their work on *Pete's Dragon* and take quick swim. For *Pete's Dragon* the studio built a huge outdoor set which was very impressive. There was an enormous hole dug in the ground of the back lot and filled with water. Around the edge of water they constructed a New England style fishing village as if the village sat on the edge of a harbor. It was very magical for it was totally believable. Very sad that a beautiful work of art like that was just bulldozed down after completion of the production. Around that time there was also a beautiful western set over on the other side of the lot. It was a small western town with Zorro's large early Spanish style home as part of the set. That set was used for the Zorro series. Later the town and Zorro's home were replaced by what is now called the Zorro Parking Structure, shades of early Jonie Mitchell, "They paved paradise and put up a parking lot". I thought I did some nice work in our *Pete's Dragon* movie but the picture wasn't very well received by the movie goers. It was released on November 3, 1977.

After *Pete's Dragon* I began work on *The Small One*, a featurette, which was a Christmas story about Joseph and Mary that Don Bluth was directing. Don had talked Ron Miller, the company President, into letting him do the picture before moving on to his next project. For the live action reference on the picture we borrowed costumes from wardrobe and a pet pony from a neighbor of one of the animators, Heidi Guidel. I played Joseph, Vera Macaluso played the Virgin Mary and the pony played a burro. Vera worked as a clean-up artist in the character department at the time. Don Hahn, who went on to produce *Beauty and the Beast, Lion King, Hunchback of Notre Dame*, and *Atlantis,* was assistant director to Don Bluth at the time. It was all great fun except for the political storm which was brewing around Don. Don wanted to run the animation department and Ron Miller, son in law of Walt himself, and President of Walt Disney Productions, didn't see it that way. And of course the guys from Cal Arts were in the mix with their own needs which were involved in the process.

During the production of *The Small One* the studio offered a trip to Disney World for those of us that had vacation time coming. It was a two week trip for fifteen hundred dollars with a one week stay at Disney World and a one week cruise in the Caribbean. It was just the adventure I needed to get me away from the studio and to put my mind in a different space from work and domestic pressures and the price was very okay. The day of departure I took my bags to the studio. There we boarded buses for the Los Angeles International Airport and were whisked away on a charter aircraft headed for Miami. I didn't see my luggage until I arrived at my room on the ninth floor of the Disney Contemporary Resort Hotel.

When I boarded the aircraft in Los Angeles I sat next to a very charming lady. As we took off for Miami the lady and I began the typical tourist conversation. The lady's name was Nancy and the ease of our conversation made me think that this lady just might have the potential to become a part of my life beyond a Caribbean cruise. As we landed in New Orleans for a stopover a man who I hadn't noticed began to stir in the seat next to Nancy. When he finally woke up and rose into my vision, Nancy turned to me and said, "Dorse, meet my husband Ross. We just got married and this is our honeymoon." My romantic dream was shattered, but Ross and Nancy became good friends of mine and we had a wonderful time on our trip.

Before this trip I had noticed a loss of hair on the back of my head, just enough to worry me so I tried a comb-over for awhile. I eventually decided that I was only fooling myself, especially in a wind, so I gave up on the comb-over and accepted the aging thing. On the Disney World trip, as Ross, Nancy and I were entering a display area from a windy out doors I pulled my comb out of my pocket and ran it through my slowly disappearing hair to make sure I looked tidy without a comb-over. Nancy, walking behind me scurried up beside me just as I put my comb back in my pocket and said something I thought very clever and funny, "Dorse, you missed a spot," thus further cementing my hair loss reality in my own mind. So Nancy did become part of my life beyond the Caribbean cruise but as a friend and Ross's wife.

The Disney people had planned parties for us every night of the first week and then for the second week we sailed the Caribbean and visited the islands. A highlight for me was visiting Haiti where six of us took a trip up to Henri Christophe's Sans-Souci Palace and the fortress, Citadelle LaFerriere. We rode in an old Land Rover type bus up into the mountains where we exchanged the Land Rover for horses and continued on horses up the narrow trail to the fortress. Henri Christophe was the leader of the slave rebellion in Haiti that won their independence from France in 1804. In 1810 he built his royal home, Sans-Souci Palace near the town of Milot not far from where the fortress would be built. He was proclaimed King Henri in 1811. He built the fortress, finished in 1820, to protect the island nation in case the French came back to re-conquer it. When Christophe was incapacitated by a stroke in 1820, insurrection broke out and the deserted King shot himself. In 1842 an earthquake devastated the city of Cap-Haitian and damaged the palace.

Of course the whole Caribbean trip was filled with all of the snorkeling, rum, boats, food, dancing, and debauchery stuff that make a Caribbean cruise what it is. But on the down side the ship broke a propeller shaft as we were heading back to Miami so that slowed the ship's speed and extended our fun trip an extra day with an open bar. That was just fine with me but soon I found myself back at the studio in my real world of animation art and artist egos.

CHAPTER 8
So I skip out Again

I was comfortable in my position as effects department supervisor at Walt Disney Feature Animation, but there were clouds forming on the animation horizon. Don Bluth, along with Gary Goldman and John Pomeroy, felt the studio wasn't being true to what they thought Walt Disney himself wanted of animation. Actually, Walt was never one to hang around after he had accomplished what he had set out to do. He succeeded with animated shorts making Mickey Mouse a world famous star, then moved on to animate the worlds first commercially successful animated feature films. Once he had that mastered he went into live action and then on to the Disneyland parks then Disney World and EPCOT, the Environmentally Planned Community of Tomorrow. Don Bluth must have wanted to continue with animation where Walt left off.

Don, Gary and John, to further their desire to follow in Walt's animation foot steps, had sat up shop in Don's garage in Culver City, California. Culver City is a town with a rich movie history which of course, is always credited to Hollywood. Don had written a script called *Banjo the Woodpile Cat* and had attracted a group of animation aficionados from Disney to help make an animated film in their spare time; they hoped to learn classical animation in the Disney style. Everyone worked for the love of the art, the fun of the project and a promise of some sort of success in the distant future. Of course, in the beginning all of the work was done in Don's garage which had been converted into a small animation studio. Remember that Walt Disney started in his garage so oddly enough that's where *Banjo the Woodpile Cat* started. Maybe a garage is a necessary first step for animation success.

The artists would arrive at Don's garage after a full day at Disney to work late into the evening and most weekends. Everyone was hoping to make a little film which would be noticed by the big world. As the tension at Disney increased, Don, John, and Gary became convinced that to carry on the Disney tradition of classical animation we would have to do it outside of Disney's. One day I had a conversation with Don about staying at Disney's because all the equipment was there, a complete animation facility. "It's just buildings", he replied, making the unspoken point that it takes people to create an animation facility, not buildings.

Eventually there was enough of *Banjo* completed to show the money people what promise we had as animators. A company called Aurora Entertainment was interested in putting up the money for a feature film. They had a connection in Chicago, a commodities broker who was interested in animation and had a lot of spare change to invest. I had just finished my work on *The Small One* and had started working on a feature film called *The Black Hole,* a live action science fiction story with animated, hand drawn, 2d effects. The production designer of the film was Peter Ellenshaw, a successful fine artist who, in 1993, was honored by the studio as a Disney Legend. The spectacular success of George Lucas's brilliant *Star Wars* inspired Walt Disney Productions to do a film which would cash in on that sci-fi success.

Don Bluth was talking about leaving the studio with John Pomeroy and Gary Goldman to do an animated film which was going to have the title of *The Secret of NIMH.* Don had mentioned that he would like for me to join them as special effects supervisor. Even though I was intrigued by Don's offer I felt I had a professional obligation to finish *The Black Hole* and was having a good time doing it. Jack Buckley had retired as effects department head and left me in charge as the animation effects department supervisor. Ted Kierscey, an effects animator, was helping me animate the laser blasts, rocket engine exhaust, and various visual effects that at the time only hand drawn 2d animation could accomplish. Don Paul was just out of the Eric Larson animation training group and he was assisting us. There was even some input from Brad Bird, later to become a successful director for Pixar Studios. During a conversation with Brad he revealed his successful directorial future when he expressed some ideas about how I might animate the laser beams when the actors fired their hi-tech weapons.

One day, as I was exiting the animation building to go across the street to the main studio theater to view the dailies, Ron Miller, the films producer and head of Walt Disney Productions, stepped out of the elevator with the same intention. Crossing the street together forced us to become a social entity. As we walked across the street I made an effort to connect with Ron. I stretched my neck and looked up, way up, for he was way over six feet tall. I raised my voice to reach up where he was and said, "Hi Ron, are we going to see some good stuff today?" Without diverting his eyes from his goal, the theater ahead, and not looking down at me, he replied with an abrupt "Well are we?" It didn't seem to be a friendly reply and sat me back a bit so I replied with a possible-positive "hope so." We walked into the theater and I sat down in the back as Ron walked on and sat down forward at the control console with a group of his chosen few. Before the dailies started rolling a guy came in and sat down next to me and introduced himself as the director, Gary Nelson. It had never occurred to me at the time but the guy that sat down next to me in that theater could have been anybody for I had never met Gary Nelson. He made comments that led me to believe that he wasn't happy with the movie. At the time I felt a kinship with the man for I wasn't happy with the movie either. I think that Gary was director in name only for Ron seemed to be the actual director since he was producer and president of the company and wanted to do it all. I sensed a lack of unity.

The Black Hole was finally finished and those in charge decided to end the movie with one of the six endings which had been written for it. Shortly after the film was in the can I received a call from Ron Miller's office and was instructed to be at a sweat box screening room in the animation studio at seven thirty the next morning. I was to view the film with Ron Miller and Eustace Lycett, the composite optical photographer; Art Cruickshank, director of miniature photography; and Bob Broughton, optical photography coordinator. Early on in the production Bob had come to me and ask if I could make some diffusion filters. He said the studio's commercial filters weren't in good shape and I could make some by spraying clear lacquer fixative on cels. He wanted me to cut cels into squares that would fit in his optical printer, then grade and number them one through ten, from slight diffusion, number one, to a barely- able-to-see-through number ten. All of the hand drawn effects we had animated for the movie—the glowing softness of the rocket engines, lasers, and various effects were created using Bob's home made filters that I had constructed for him. Years later, in 2001, Bob was honored as a Disney Legend for his extensive camera and optical work on most all of the Disney animated features including *Pinocchio* and *Snow White and the Seven Dwarfs* as well as *The Black Hole*.

Well there I was with the big guys. In that pecking order I was the lowest; there was no one under me to peck. There was Joe Hale who had worked on the picture as liaison between live action and animated effects, but he didn't show up that morning. Come to think of it, he was supposed to be above me in the film's pecking order. He received a screen credit for director of animated special effects but wasn't there to support me. Even though our animation department did the hand drawn animated effects in the picture Joe took all the credit for our work and got his name and picture in the publicity magazines.

Ouch, ego damage! The studio didn't give me my due credit because I had resigned from the studio right after the picture was finished so I could join the newly formed Don Bluth Productions. Walt Disney Studio rewrote history for publicity and said Joe Hale had animated the effects. In fact an article about the animated effects for *The Black Hole* appeared in Starlog Magazine. It had a heading which read "The magic is in the pencil of Joe Hale." Hey, it was my pencil! Well, a lot of it was my pencil and some it was Ted Keirscey's and Don Paul's and a few other people. None of it was Joe Hale's pencil.

The morning of *The Black Hole* screening I was very nervous because I was the only peasant present and wondered what I was doing there. The lights went down, the movie rolled and we all sat quietly as the film fumbled its way to the end. The lights came up and there was that long awkward pause, everyone waiting for someone to say something. Every one of the big guys looked at me, why I don't know unless they didn't want to have to tell Ron that his film was a piece of crap knock off of Star Wars. Ron Miller turned to me, peon of peons, and said "Dorse, what do you think of it?" Gee, my mind was going nowhere a mile a minute. Here I was with the son-in-law of Walt Disney and the Producer of the film and I thought his movie was a disaster. I really thought *The Black Hole* would be a black eye for the studio. It seemed like forever before I managed to get some words formed in my head. I wanted to weigh my words carefully. I couldn't just blurt out how I felt for that would have made me sound like a crazy person. Since the film was in the can and I had never been invited to any production meetings I thought I was just there to offer support, a yes man kind of thing. The fact that I had decided to quit the studio to join Bluth was momentarily blocked out by my intense sense of survival. I could have said "Ron, this movie is a classic science fiction film adventure and the youthful theater public who inhabit the movie houses will love it." But no, I didn't say that, I didn't believe that. I finally sputtered something like "Well, the good guys won." It was a totally inane comment and I was embarrassed by uttering it. Still am. That moment was one of my most uncomfortable moments at the Walt Disney Studios. That experience caused a short circuit in my memory much like blacking out in a car wreck. I don't recall what happened after that. I just remember it was a great relief to get out of that screening room and be on my way.

Finally Don, John and Gary secured financial backing for their feature film *The Secret of NIMH*. Don had bought the rights to a Newberry Award winning children's book, *Mrs. Frisby and the Rats of NIMH* by Robert C. O'Brien. The film we made, based on this book, is a story about a mouse named Mrs. Brisby who is trying to save her small son Timmy from a serious illness and in the process meets up with an advanced rat culture which has learned to use electricity. The rat culture is not entirely altruistic because it steals the electricity from the neighborhood farmer. In the movie version, the name of Mrs. Frisby had to be changed to Mrs. Brisby due to legal forces, I was told, from the people who made the Frisbee toy, which is not the same spelling as Frisby with a y, but who really knows why. It was never explained to me why O'brien could use the name Frisby with a Y instead of an EE in his book but we couldn't use it in the film. So with the name problem solved, me confused, and financial backing in place, Don quit The Walt Disney Company on his birthday, September 1979. John, Gary, Lorna Pomeroy, Vera Macaluso, Heidi Guidel, Diann Landau, Dave Spafford, Skip Jones, Linda Miller, Sally Voorhies and Emily Juliano, all left the studio with Don. There was much political haggling in Disney's animation department at the time, with several ex Cal Arts students competing with Don Bluth for the power position, whatever that was. The three, Don, John, and Gary, knew the time was now. It was the talk of the studio and made the front page of the New York Times. A picture of all of them in the back of Gary's Toyota pickup truck accompanied the article. The exodus set back the production of *The Fox and Hound* six months. It turned out to be a bigger deal than anyone anticipated.

The original rebels

The next day Ron Miller called a meeting of all the remaining animators. We were to meet in his conference room at two thirty that afternoon. The whole studio was talking about the mass resignation. I hadn't revealed my future resignation because I had just finished working on *The Black Hole*, so I had to join the meeting. Every one was seated around the very big walnut conference table waiting for the King, Ron, to enter. There was excitement in the air. With Don and his entourage gone the political playing field had been leveled a bit. Ron entered the room late but no one was going to call him on it. Not only was he head of The Walt Disney Company, a much bigger entity than the animation department, he was a six foot four inch former professional football player, a very tanned, hansom, formidable figure. He sat down at the head of the very large, polished walnut table, paused for a moment, and said, "Well, now that the cancer has been cut out..." All my friends who I thought were attempting to save the art of classical animation had just been called a cancer by the head of Walt Disney Productions and the greatest animation studio in history. Wow. The statement was so off the wall I don't remember anything after that. I'm sure the idea of the meeting was a to be a morale building effort but my brain circuits all blew at once after hearing such a strange beginning to what was to be odd meeting. After some group babbling and power struggling attempts the meeting was adjourned. It seemed everyone was excited about a nervous new beginning for the studio. With that troublemaker Don and his buddies gone there would be more creative room for the artist left behind.

The day had finally arrived for me to announce my resignation from the studio. Don was ready for me to begin on *Banjo the Woodpile Cat.* He was going to pay me fifty dollars a week more than I was making at Disney, bringing my pay up to seven hundred fifty dollars a week. A couple years earlier I had talked to Don Duckwall, the administrator over the other administrators, and ask him for a forty per cent raise in pay. He said, "That's never been done before at this studio." My reply was, "Don, there have been many first at this studio, stereophonic sound tracks, full color cartoons, so we could make this another first." He looked askance at me with a raised eyebrow and said he would talk to the other people. As a result I received a pay raise of twenty per cent. That made me happy until Bluth had the fun idea of leaving the studio, starting a company, and risking our very livelihoods in an attempt to make a successful animated feature film. After a few days of contemplation I decided it was time to take that leap of faith. I had written a long heart-felt letter of resignation which I was going to present to Ed Hanson, the animation administrator. The morning was at hand. It was a chilly, wintry, November day. I called Ed and asked if we could talk. He was open to it so I bounced into his office with a "Good morning Ed!" I was all excited about what was to be Dorse's next big adventure and handed the envelope to Ed. He opened it, pulled out my very long letter and began to silently read my brilliant good bye.

November 8, 1979
Ron Miller/Art Stevens/Ed Hansen
Walt Disney Productions
500 South Buena Vista Street Burbank, California 91521

Gentlemen;
   For starters, I have to say, this decision I have made has
come after much thought and arrived at with great difficulty.
I have decided to resign from Walt Disney Productions
effective Friday, November 23, 1979. I am writing this letter,
as opposed to a short statement because of the deep feelings I
have for Walt Disney Productions and for what I think Walt
Disney was trying to do with the art of animation.
   I don't want to sound as if I think there's no one at the
studio wanting to make "Disney films". I just think that the
fate of the animated feature at Walt Disney Productions
rests in the hands of people who have an understanding of
animation and a reverence for Walt Disney, for his attempt at
perfection and for what he did with the animated film.
   This is not to say we should be "living in the past",

I continued on and on with a very long letter which Ed continued to read without looking up. I had made what I thought were many good suggestions about how to improve the development of talent at the studio so as to continue creating the great animated films that Walt Disney was known for.

Ed very quietly finished reading the letter and as he lowered the letter he raised his eyes to meet mine and said, "Dorse, you'd better get out of the studio, Ron's coming in this afternoon and he's going to be upset." I mumbled something about a two week notice and he said, "Never mind that! Just get out of the studio."

Gee, not even thanks for all the good work I had done, I felt like such a heel. My letter, as I read it now, was a bit over the top but I was caught up in the conflicting personalities of the period. I was trying too hard to make a point.

Since Disney didn't respect my

Ed Hansen waves good bye

two-week notice I had two paid weeks to kick back before going to work with Don Bluth Productions. My friend Nancy, from the Caribbean trip, worked at Disneyland and she invited me to join a group of Disneyland employees planning a trip to go river-rafting down the Green River in Utah, a perfect getaway from the tumult of the past few weeks. The group had charter buses pick us up at the studio. There were just a couple of us from the studio, the rest were Disneyland employees. We rode the buses from Burbank to Utah, stopping to camp overnight in Zion National Park. The next day we went on up through Bryce Canyon National Park to the town of Green River, Utah. At the time that town was a one intersection, one stoplight town, which had been a real estate effort in the 40's. It's in the middle of nowhere but the area has many dinosaur quarries, ancient American Indian ruins, and the history of the old west. There was a small airport with a small, beat up corrugated tin building for a hanger and bumpy dirt runway.

At sunrise, after camping overnight, we made our way to the aircraft parked at the end of the runway. There were five, Cessna 172's, and each would hold a pilot and three passengers. Nancy, Ross and I piled into one of the planes with our sleeping bags and tooth brushes. Off we went bouncing down the rough dirt runway into the morning sun with a pilot at the controls whose skills we didn't question. Today I would wonder about the pilot. I guess as we age we gain the wisdom which causes us to question that which may not be as safe as a person of reason would want it to be, but we were younger then. Up, up and away we flew, flying over the barren Utah terrain with the Green River snaking a few thousand feet below us.

Our destination was ninety miles away and staring out the window all I could see was a very barren, moon-like, landscape below. After flying for about an hour the pilot began his descent down to what looked to me like a place that would only allow airplanes to crash. The pilot brought the plane down on top of what might be called a butte or mesa, which was formed when the river carved the land down around it. When we hit the ground the plane bumped and bounced on a nonexistent runway of dirt and rocks finally settling to a dusty stop. We collected our gear, thanked the pilot for not crashing, and headed down the trail, actually climbed down the cliffs, to the river. The pilot gave his engine the full throttle and lifted his aircraft off the mesa and swooped down, hot dog style, over the edge and out of sight.

When we finally got on the rafts and floated off down the river in the middle of the absolutely nowhere northern Utah, I suddenly felt very claustrophobic, almost panicked. It was a beautiful, sunny, clear, morning but there wasn't much room to move around on the raft. I just had to sit there in the stillness staring at the desolate landscape with the walls of the canyon looming ever larger in the distance while this rubber boat just slowly glided along to what seemed to be more of nowhere. Now that I had stopped traveling, moving, and had time to notice myself I realized the past several months had filled me with great angst. I thought seven days of this inside my head stuff and I would be in a straight jacket, if anyone would have thought to bring one along. After awhile I began to feel like the cartoon character that turns red from the top down when getting angry. Sort of like Ed Hansen did when he read my letter of resignation but I was slowly turning a cool peaceful color instead of red, as the tenseness was melting away. I began to notice I was having a great time and the five of us on the raft, including the raft oarsman, were in awe of the splendid scenery on either side of the river. The funny cigarettes and ten cases of beer stored on the raft didn't hurt either. Our total group had four rafts sliding down the river as if in a parade. Indian ruins, water fights, great food, campfires, sing alongs, sleeping out under the stars, and just enough white water to make it exciting. It took seven days to float back to the town of Green River. It turned out to be a great trip, but was way too short.

Vera took care of my plants in my apartment while I was gone. We had become very close and the big lonely void in my personal life was filled with her supporting company and great sense of humor. When I returned home I found a letter that she had left for me. In the letter she said that the money people had thrown a party at a fancy house on Toluca Lake for all of the artists of Don Bluth Productions. She thought the artists were all being treated like the goose that laid the golden egg. She said she was frightened by the uproar that had been caused by the group leaving Disney and the article on the front page of the New York Times was disconcerting. She hadn't expected the Disney exodus, of which she was a part, to make such a splash.

Vera had started working for Disney's after she had learned to work as a clean up artist while working with Don Bluth on *Banjo the Wood Pile Cat*. Her path to a career in animation started when she had a job doing needle point designs and had met the sister of Lorna Pomeroy. Lorna was a Disney animator, working with Don Bluth on *Banjo*. Lorna's sister told Vera that Lorna was helping some people that were working in a garage on an animated film. They would teach animation to any artist interested. Vera had always liked cartoon animation so she made a call and ended up working with Don during evenings and weekends learning the art of animation.

The darling duo, Lorna and Vera

This led her to a day job at Hana Barbera. When Don found out she was at Hana Barbera he said he would hire her at Disney's, so she resigned from Hanna Barbera and was hired into the clean up department at Disney.

I was happy to be starting my new position with Don Bluth Productions and happy with my work on *The Black Hole*. One of the first things I did for Don Bluth Productions was make two sets of home-made Bob Broughton diffusion filters. Those filters helped to create some of the magic in our first Don Bluth feature, *The Secret of NIMH*.

The Black Hole opened on December 21, 1979, two weeks after *Star Trek: The Motion Picture*. *The Black Hole* wasn't a successful picture, even with the nice effects using my home-made filters, but even to this day there are a few sci-fi cult fans around who praise the film as a favorite.

Don Bluth Productions was planning to screen a rough-cut of *Banjo the Woodpile Cat*. All of those long hours of hard work had produced enough film footage for a crew screening. It was planned as a first get together of the new crew so everyone could see the film and become aware of how much work we had to do to finish the picture. The night of the screening I drove to Hollywood from my apartment in Burbank. I pulled into the dark parking lot across the street from the theater. As I walked out of the darkness toward the crowd of artists in front of the theater everyone started cheering me as if I were the Holy Savior. They were very happy that I had decided to join the new company as the Special Effects Supervisor. We all knew we were out on a limb and we would need each other's total support to make this dream come true.

A few weeks later Don Bluth sponsored me for membership in the Academy of Motion Picture Arts and Sciences. Ed Hansen was on the board of the Academy; my application was rejected.

CHAPTER 9
A Well oiled career Ahead

I began working on *Banjo the Woodpile Cat* in San Gabriel, California, at Fred Craig's house. He had space for me to work which wasn't available at Don's house because everyone else on the movie was working there. Fred and his wife Olga had an animation Xerox business. The method of copying a drawing to a transparent, celluloid sheet, or cel, by hand inking them, had been replaced with a Xerox machine. Bluth talked Fred into joining us on the *Banjo* project. Don's house was full of animation desks and the garage had been turned into the ink and paint department. Even though Xerox was being used to transfer drawings to cels it was still called the ink and paint department.

Working long days and many weekends we finally completed the animation. We all pitched in and painted cels, cleaned cels, and did whatever else that needed to be done. By the end of the project we were all at Don's house, working through the night, taking turns helping on the camera housed in the front garage, shooting the last few scenes before the deadline. As one moved through Don's house, which by this time was completely taken over by the project, there were people sleeping under desks and where ever else they could get some rest before waking to take their turn on whatever needed to be done. It was a marathon finish which went around the clock for several days. The morning the camera crew shot the last scene I stopped for a break and fell asleep on a cot in the back yard. I opened my eyes to sunshine as Vera awakened me and said the film was finished. This meant all of the animation and art had been put on film and now those reels of film had to be edited into a movie. We were over the big hurdle with many hurdles to come.

Don Bluth Productions had leased a building in Studio City for our new studio, but we had to wait until it was vacant before we could move in. In the meantime Don and a few people worked at his house developing a screenplay for what was to be *The Secret of NIMH*. Don wanted Vera and me to search the countryside to find a particular kind of farm tractor. It was to be used as a model for the sequence in the film where the farmers plow threatens Mrs. Brisby's cinder block house. The tractor design was the type which had the two small wheels in front, set on an angle to fit into the groove, or furrow, which the plow would make on its last plow through. Don was going to film the tractor and process the film to make it fit with the animation. Vera and I toured the farms of California from Oxnard to San Diego looking for a tractor which nobody seemed to use anymore. We met all kinds of interesting people but didn't find the tractor. We even found a farm implement museum in a farmer's barn down in the hills outside of San Diego. We made an appointment with the farmer who owned the place and drove down there on a cold rainy day. The farmer accompanied us out to the barn, a musty old mausoleum for the forgotten farm tools. The barn was full of wonderful old rusty tractors and plows but the tractor we were looking for wasn't there. Don finally found one on a trip which he took back to Utah to visit relatives. He filmed the tractor there and brought back the film. Vera and I were no longer looking for a tractor and the studio didn't have a building so I retreated to my apartment in Burbank and started writing a book about effects animation. Before I had finished the book, an exercise which taught me how little I knew about writing a book, we moved into our new building in Studio City. After that my life became a whirlwind of animation and the book was never finished.

Our 1980 Studio City home, Don Bluth Productions with my 280 ZX in the parking lot.

Studio City, California, 1980. Don Bluth Productions moved into the new digs, the rear building of a two-story building complex on Ventura Boulevard. The front building, on the boulevard, housed an Imperial Savings and Loan on the ground-floor and an Iranian restaurant upstairs.

Our new studio had balconies on the second floor. The north side looked out on the concrete wash which runs through Studio City to the L.A. River. On the south side of the building the balcony looked down on a very large courtyard patio, shared with the front building, with a fountain and benches for relaxing in the sun. We had our own parking lot by the wash and there were lots of restaurants in the neighborhood as well as shops of all sorts. Having such a nice new studio in such a handy little city helped us to feel more secure about our decision to start an animated feature with just over a dozen artists, a major project which would eventually provide jobs for several hundred people over the course of the next year or so.

When we first moved into the building all of the studio furniture which Don, John and Gary, had acquired was stored in one of the largest ground-floor rooms. It would have to stay there until we could assign space to people and get things organized. The first morning we were all present, I think there was about sixteen of us, the sun was shining, the sky was clear, a beautiful spring morning. Don called a meeting of our little group and as we all huddled in one corner of a large vacant room, facing Don, he began by saying, "Today we are all aboard a tiny dinghy, in the middle of the ocean, and we must find land." Thus began a fun-filled, grueling, exhausting, rewarding, painful, wonderful, agonizing year of making an animated feature film. Don, John, and Gary, surrounded by stacks of how to write screenplay books, started the arduous task of turning the book, *Mrs. Frisby and the Rats of NIMH,* into a screenplay with proper plot points and character arcs while the rest of the studio started thinking about their respective jobs for the production.

"Dorse, we need to have a scale model of the interior of Mrs. Brisby's house. A model the layout artist can use to do their layout drawings. You can get started building it." Don had given me my first art assignment for *The Secret of NIMH*: a large three-foot by three-foot scale model, with a staircase and fireplace, all faux painted to look as if it was made of tree branches and stone.

I must say it turned out rather well. By the time I had finished it we had a few scenes ready for effects animation. I was happy to start drawing again and still remember the first scene I was given to animate. It was a scene of an underground shot in the mole hole where the moles are disturbed by the dirt falling in on them because the rabbits above are stamping out an alert to warn of the farmer's tractor approach. Before I finished the scene my work was

Showing my completed model to John, Don, and Gary.

interrupted by *Xanadu,* a live action romantic romp of a film starring Olivia Newton John and Gene Kelly. The producers of that film wanted Don Bluth Productions to animate a two-minute romantic punctuation for the middle of the picture. Don decided we would take a small crew to his house and spend three months, twelve hours a day, seven days a week, working in the garage. It would bring in a little early revenue for the fledgling Don Bluth Productions and the overtime money would help me pay for my new sports car, a Datsun 280 ZX. (The Datsun Company later became Nissan.) Don was going to animate the character stuff and I would animate the affects. We had already hired Bruce Heller as an effects assistant. Bruce knew film in and out and was also a licensed pyrotechnician. Bruce always worked standing at his desk, never sitting down. We brought along Diann Landau to assist with the effects. She was a special effects artist and one of the original group of artists to resign from Disney. We added a few more artists as the animation progressed so after a few weeks the garage was fairly stuffed with people.

Those days in Culver City were a strange mixture of delirium and delight. It was the early summer and the garage had no air conditioning. Don did have a swimming pool in the back yard so each afternoon a few of us, usually Bruce and I, would spend 10 minutes jumping off the garage roof into the cooling waters of the pool. After the break we would go back to work in our wet bathing apparel and work until dinner time. Don had hired a cook, a sweet lady of some European extraction well versed in the culinary arts. She was to prepare lunch and dinner for the crew so no one would have to wander off to find a restaurant at meal time.

It was a very stressful period and after awhile the long hours began to wear on everyone. One day Diann took a walk around the block for a little relief and came back with her knees all banged up. She said someone had pushed her down. Someone she didn't see, there was no one around but it felt like "someone pushed me." The story seemed stress related. My stress caught up with me one morning as I was driving to work in my fancy, speedy, sports car. I noticed everyone on the Ventura Freeway was going much too fast. I muttered to myself, "What's wrong with these people?" Everyone was passing me on the left and on the right. I finally made it to work after what seemed like hours. The trip was usually an eighty mile an hour, very early morning no traffic, twenty minute trip, Burbank to Culver City, but that day it seemed to take forever. When I finally arrived at work I was totally torpid. I couldn't accomplish anything. That afternoon I told Don that I felt like my soul had been sucked out of me, I felt empty, drained. I had never felt that way and it worried me. I said I was going home. I drove back to Burbank in a daze, carefully parked my car in my assigned space and crawled up the stairs to my studio apartment. I went to bed, promptly fell asleep, slept for about twelve hours, and woke up the next morning feeling fine, zipped off to work in my ZX, eighty miles an hour, Culver City in twenty minutes. I was totally fine that day and have never felt that tired or soul-less since. The *Xanadu* animation was eventually completed without any serious injuries. After the film was finished those of us who had worked on the animation went to the crew screening. We cheered and clapped with all of the dancers and actors from the movie as we celebrated the film, relieved to have it over with.

We moved out of Don's garage and back to Studio City and joined the rest of the crew working on *The Secret of NIMH*. It was nice to get back to Studio City and Art's Deli, a great Jewish delicatessen across Ventura Boulevard from the studio. We placed our desks and tables throughout the building. We each had lots of room but as the production proceeded and more artists were hired the building became quite cozy. I started out in one of the large rooms upstairs. That room was also occupied by the layout department and background department, the layout department being Larry Leeker and the background department being Don Moore. Eventually, as these departments hired artists I was moved downstairs to what must originally have been a closet with a window, a very small, six-foot by eight-foot room in the northwest corner of the building.

It had a floor to ceiling window the width of the room which looked out on the parking lot. By the time I had my desk, chair and a table, stuffed into the room there was barely enough room for me. To give me another six inches of room I had to design a shelf that held the stacks of scenes on an angle, about six inches deep, instead of on top of each other twelve inches deep, an all around, talented, Randy Fullmer, built that shelf for me.

All of the customers who came to use the neighborhood bank or the Iranian restaurant had to circle the building on the way out of the parking lot and would drive by my window no more than four feet from me. I was surprised one day when a car stopped at the window and the pretty lady driver in the car starred at me and waved. She was my dental hygienist who happened to recognize me in my little room. It was a small world moment outside the window of my small room. I had my two animators, Diann and Bruce in the next room between my room and the hallway, so I had to pass through their room to get into my room. Later on we hired Tom Hush as an effects animator and had to put him in the hallway outside Diann and Bruce's room. Things were getting crowded.

My Studio City Secret of NIMH work room

Don Bluth again sponsored me for membership in the Academy of Motion Picture Arts and Sciences. This time I was accepted.

CHAPTER 10

oops, Who Took the FUN out of FUNdiNg

Up on the second floor of our building, Don, John and Gary continued the struggle of making a book into a screenplay. Will Finn and Steven Barnes were brought in to help. Don was story boarding as they went so the production was progressing from book to screenplay to storyboards to layouts to animation. We had a lot of artists eager to get started so Don had to start handing out scenes as soon as he had completed a section of the story. People were learning to draw the characters and everyone was experimenting in their own specialty. Eventually enough of the story was completed that people could begin to work in their assigned departments.

Work was now flowing through the studio and some of it was now ending up on film. Joe Juliano was the camera department, and his animation camera crane was setup in a room across the hall from my little two room suite with Diann and Bruce. This made it very handy for Joe and me to consult on the effects as we were working on the movie. Joe is a curious and talented creature. He had designed a large painting machine which he had built in his garage. There were airbrushes on long sliding arms which were controlled by a computer. Joe could program the machine to paint an abstract work of art of his own design, very impressive. Joe is a problem solver. For the main title of *The Secret of NIMH* I wanted the flames to appear to be more magical than just flames so I ask Joe if we could do a second exposure pass through the camera and truck in on each frame. I wanted the flames to radiate light beams out at the screen. Joe rigged up stops, using paper clips, on the camera crane so as he placed the flame art under the camera to shoot one frame he would also start the camera trucking down to a smaller field. The stops he had installed on the camera crane would trip open the shutter when the camera started to truck down, at precisely the right time, and close it when the camera had completed the move. This would smear the back light flame matte on the film frame and make it appear as light radiating out from the flames. For the second exposure of that frame the back-lit flame matte would be exposed without trucking. This double exposure would make it appear that the flames were radiating light outward. Compared to today's technology this effort was a very clever, simple, and primitive solution, but it worked for us.

To keep track of the animation as it flowed through the studio, Joe, with the help of David Steinberg, designed a computer program to keep track of all the scenes required for *The Secret of NIMH*. David Steinberg, a college film student, came from Chicago to work with us during his summer vacations. The program Joe and David wrote ran on a Radio Shack TRS 80 computer with sixty four kilobytes, a very small, weakly powered computer compared to all of those in the homes today and this one I'm typing on right now which is five hundred twelve megabytes, and it's an old one.

Everything was running smoothly at Don Bluth Productions and Vera and I had been dating for awhile. We were thinking that we would be together forever so we decided that it would simplify our lives if were living together. She had a small apartment over on Buena Vista in Burbank and we thought it would be good for her to move into my more fully-furnished one bedroom at Lakeside Apartments in Burbank. After living in my apartment for awhile and feeling secure in our jobs Vera and I started thinking about the possibility of buying a house. We found a nice little house for sale in North Hollywood, not far from Lakeside Apartments.

The North Hollywood house

Vera and I made a deal to buy the house by going in together on the down payment, two-thirds for me and one third for her. I had received a stock option from Disney which I sold when I resigned to go with Don Bluth Productions, so I had a little more money saved than Vera.

We worked on *The Secret of NIMH* many weekends and many evenings. Vera was the supervisor of the clean up department which was an enormous task but she still found time to help me with the effects. We worked one long weekend dry brushing the mattes used for backlighting the effects created when, at the beginning of the film, Nicodemus is introduced as he magically writes in his book and signs his name. Everyone was working long hours weekdays and weekends. Don Bluth Productions had a finite amount of money and a finite amount of time but the work required for an animated feature seemed infinite. The company had become a huge collection of artists. The building so cramped more space had to be rented in the neighboring buildings. The deadline was looming ever closer.

As a break for the crew, and to relieve the stress of long work hours, the company decided to go to Catalina for a weekend. Every one stayed at the Bay View Hotel in Avalon. Well, everyone except Vera and I. We had decided to get married on Catalina Island that weekend. Vera had made arrangements with the justice of the peace for a Saturday morning wedding in the courtyard behind Avalon's little court house. Our wedding was to be a secret ceremony except for witnesses, Don Bluth, John and Lorna Pomeroy, and a production executive, Mel Griffin. Vera invited Dave Spafford, a character animator at

Gary and the Bluth Group checking into the Bay View Hotel

Don Bluth and friends have a Catalina breakfast

the time, to film the wedding with his super eight motion picture camera. We didn't have digital video in those days but Dave thought his "super eight" was very advanced for home movies. The Friday boat trip over to Catalina was not revealing, that is, no one seemed to know what Vera and I had planned for the weekend. We were very good about keeping a very exciting secret.

After the boat docked we collected our belongings and took the short walk into town. Vera and I checked into Scaris Hotel, rather than the Bay View Hotel, where our friends would be staying

Vera and I wanted to be apart from the crowd that weekend for our wedding mischief. The next morning Avalon, being a tiny town, was fairly sprinkled with friends from work.

As Vera and I walked down the beachfront boulevard of Avalon toward the court house, we met a few friends who offered to hang out with us, but we politely declined. We arrived at the courthouse and as we took care of the paperwork the few friends we had invited began to arrive. With so few people at our wedding it could only be described as dainty but the California setting in the courtyard was romantic and of course Avalon is a magical, romantic place, The Beach Boys said so. Vera and I assumed our getting married positions and the justice of the peace did his officiating. One moment a couple of single people and the next moment, with a few simple words from a state official, a married couple, bound for life. Everyone cheered with hugs and kisses all around. The word quickly got around Avalon that Dorse

John and Don have an early morning swim

and Vera had gotten married that day. That evening Don Bluth Productions had a barbeque at the Bay View Hotel and announced that Vera and I were husband and wife. All of our co worker friends were there, spewing with glee for Vera and me, as they packed into the courtyard patio. I picked up Vera and paraded around the hotel patio, in front of everyone, as if I had won a prize at the fair. One of the guys, a very talented Terrie Eddings, played a beautiful love song on the recorder and the evening was on. The rest of the weekend was spent with the typical Catalina activities, swimming at Desconso Beach, snorkeling, glass bottom boating, with Dave Spafford recording all of it for a film history.

Vera and I were eager to see the film footage Spafford shot of our wedding but by the time he showed it to us he had erased the sound track and cut the footage into the rest of the film he had shot that weekend. He added a sound track of Elvis Pressley singing The Hawaiian Wedding Song over our wedding shots. Vera and I never received a copy of the film. That was a bit bizarre for Vera had invited Dave to our wedding for the express purpose of filming the ceremony for us. But that no longer matters. Well, yes it does.

After that weekend and the jolt back to reality that returning home presented, *The Secret of NIMH* began to take shape. It looked as if Don Bluth Productions was going to have our first animated feature film in the can. The word was that the money people would finance two more films if *The Secret of NIMH* did well. The movie was released on July 2, 1982, with a roll out plan. That is, it starts in theaters on one coast, and rolls out to the other, depending on how well the film is doing. One Saturday morning Vera and I went to a theater in North Hollywood where our film was playing. We were excited and curious to see how it was doing. As we walked up to the theater there was a crowd of scruffy looking youths waiting to get into the theatre, but after close inspection we found they weren't there to see *The Secret of NIHM*. They were waiting in line for the latest Ralph Bakshi film, *American Pop*. There was a couple, shuffling about with their pre teen kids, attempting to chose a movie to see. One of the kids pointed to the display poster of our movie to which the mother quickly responded with, "No, that's a Disney movie." Vera and I both felt a twinge of pain but we were at least happy to have *The Secret of NIMH* thought of as a Disney movie. We felt that was some kind of satisfaction. Our movie didn't do well in the theaters and that cast a pall of doubt about the future for all of us at Don Bluth Productions.

To celebrate our third wedding anniversary, Vera and I planned to have dinner at Mikados Restaurant in North Hollywood. It is a nice Japanese restaurant with lots of parking on the front side of the building. Vera and I had driven my car to work that day and I was low on gas so when we were ready to go out I suggested taking Vera's Porsche.

We hadn't driven it for awhile and it was a fun little car and had more gas than mine. We parked just a few steps from the restaurant entrance and had a nice table where I presented a card and gift to Vera. When we had finished dinner and taken care of the tab we moseyed out of the restaurant to find a Mercedes parked where we had left Vera's Porsche. It was one of those real life what's wrong with this picture moments. We finally recaptured our senses

A 1979 Porsche 912e similar to the one Vera owned

and telephoned the police but of course the car was gone and that was that. We were very despondent and spent many weeks driving around the valley looking for it. Several weeks later the police called and said they had the car in a junk yard in L.A. It had been found in the brush off the 2 freeway, stripped. Vera and I had to go identify it. The car was a mess of wreckage and Vera cried and cried and cried all the way home. She loved that car and she felt a great loss. The insurance company paid us well for it so we bought a Datsun 280 ZX sports car for Vera. Now we had matching sports cars. It didn't help the sadness of losing the Porsche but one has to move on and moving on in nice sport car isn't bad, but of course it wasn't a Porsche.

The people who were going to fund two more films for Don Bluth Productions if *The Secret of NIMH* did well were not happy with the film's weak public response. We at Don Bluth Productions began to wonder if we would have another project to keep all of us employed. Would we be out in the street? I was wondering, who took the fun out of funding? Hoping for the best, Vera and I had constructed plans to take a ten day Caribbean cruise with John and Lorna Pomeroy. Lorna was a talented animator and had married John a few years earlier. With the news looking grim, John and Lorna decided to cancel their part of the cruise but Vera and I thought, gee, without a job we wouldn't have to take time off work. We decided to go ahead with the cruise and had a wonderful time. We met many wonderful people, snorkeled in some amazing waters, enjoyed every minute and never worried or wondered if we would have a job when we got back to the real world. But back at the studio people had been worrying.

CHAPTER 11

The My$tery MoNey MaN PROMi$ed MillioN$

After that depressing period of worry and wonder the studio was saved from disaster when Don Bluth Productions had the good fortune to connect with some people interested in doing an innovative new approach to the video game. The game machine, history's first 2d animated video game, would use an animated cartoon, in color, on a laser disk.

It was the first video game to use hand drawn cel animation for the graphics. Different sequences of the cartoon could be accessed by the use of a joystick that directed the laser beam to the proper point in the game. The player would attempt to direct the story by using the joy stick to pick the next scene which would advance the character's action to save one's self from some sort of innovative destruction. The hero would then be faced with another challenge to be saved again until he died the assigned number of deaths or succeeded to the end of the game. We were very fortunate to get this project.

Studying the fire matte for the video game with Dirk the Daring

Without money to do an animated film we were very close to being out of business.

While we were working on the laser disc games a gentleman came to the studio and introduced himself as a person interested in financing Don Bluth Productions. Every one was very excited, it would mean financing for future films, exactly what we needed if we were going to continue getting paid. The video games would only last so long and we had just gone through a terribly frightening period after *The Secret of NIMH* backers failed to finance another feature. I wasn't a participant in the many, many, on going meetings and phone calls, which involved this mystery person, but we all knew what was going on. It was just too exciting to keep it quiet. The mystery man would come to the studio in an old "hard top" Cadillac which had the covering on the hard top peeled off, exposing the bare metal. He seemed to know of all the available real estate in southern California which could be converted into an animation studio, big places, such as the elementary school in La Cresenta which was for sale. Wow! We thought our luck had turned. It was too good to be true.

The mystery man also had an interest in helping our studio survive so we could become a big competitive threat to Walt Disney Productions. It seems that it was alleged, or we had heard, or somebody said, this person had been involved in a business deal with Ron Miller, at that time president of Walt Disney Productions and Mr. Miller had somehow taken advantage of him and he wanted retribution. That was the story I had heard and of course I have no idea if it was true. But the man's story was that he thought his wishes for revenge could be granted by Don Bluth Productions if he could finance a studio for us and thereby pose a threat to Ron Miller. We would have a studio and his payback would be exacted. It was sounding better all the time but more like a movie plot that a dream come true.

The large amounts of money needed to fulfill the mystery man's promises were just a phone call away. He had an international deal cooking which would bring millions of dollars into his control; it was some kind of deal involving very large amounts of gold. He would call from London to say he was just hours away from signing but then he would disappear for weeks. Another phone call from New York to say this was it. He would have the money the next day. Oddly enough he seemed to know a lot of important people who had been indirectly involved with Don Bluth Productions in the financial end of things. This calling from all over the world and then disappearing went on for months. We were finishing the video games and the end of our jobs was again closing in on us. Of course, with the mystery man so convincing, there was no need to search out other financing for the company. He was good,

New Years Eve 1983, Don Bluth Productions party

and the closer he said he was to the big bucks the closer we were, as a studio, to being out of business.

Everyone in the studio began to wonder about the authenticity of the mystery man. We wanted very much to believe but as time went on it seemed more and more like the old adage, "If it sounds too good to be true it most likely is" too good to be true. We began to speculate as to what might be the truth. Early on I had wondered if the mystery backer had been hired by Ron Miller to string Don Bluth Productions along until we ran out of money. All of the information came to me second or third hand but it seemed that this was the most obvious scenario for that's what was happening. If one hears hoof beats it's probably a horse.

New Years Eve, December 31, we had a party to celebrate a successful 1983.

We had finished the work for the video games, *Dragon's Lair* and *Space Ace,* and were well into *Dragon's Lair II.* Our party was a black tie event with four hundred guests invited to the Biltmore Hotel in downtown Los Angeles with the famous Les Brown's band playing for our dancing pleasure. We all looked beautiful, glowing with our success.

Vera with one of the early Disney escapees, our editor, Jeff Patch, and me

Don toasted the evening with "Here's to money galore in '84." We were on our way, but little did we know that it was not on our way up but on our way out.

By March of 1984 the money people who were financing the video games pulled out. The day the studio got the news Don Bluth called everyone down to the lobby for an announcement. The planned meeting generated a buzz of excitement for it could be good or bad; no one knew what was up. When we had gathered in the lobby and all of us were glowing with anticipation, Don called for quiet. His announcement was short and very terse, "Everyone go home, we have run out of money." That was very harsh. Don could be an eloquent speaker when he was selling but that day he wasn't selling anything. He was announcing a death. It was quite a shock to everyone. Kathleen "Katy" Quaife, (at Bluth's we always lovingly called her Katy), an effects animator, happened to take that Friday off to visit a loan company to convince them that she had a great job and they could loan her some money, without risk, to buy an automobile. She acquired the loan but the next day, Saturday, she got a call from Diann Landau. Diann's first words were "Katy, don't bother coming to work Monday." Of course the rest of the conversation was Katy interrogating Diann to find out why she no longer had a job. As Don pulled down the curtain, another one of the artists, Kris, turned in a flash and ran upstairs to call Disney to see if there was an opening for her. Everyone else looked at each other in stunned silence and slowly, zombie like, proceeded to exit the building. I drove home with a passenger that was in tears. Vera seemed convinced that this was the end of the world. I kept my fear buried inside. I was busy driving.

The mystery money man who was going to save our studio and put us on the road to success was never heard from again. The truth no doubt shall never be ours to know but the mystery man with the promise of millions of dollars in gold stopped calling and disappeared from sight forever. Gee, maybe he got rubbed out by the gold dealers he was wooing. The studio was coming to an end faster than most of us realized.

Vera and I kept busy that summer doing freelance. We helped on each other's projects. She was more in demand than I and felt very lucky to find an occasional job to carry us along. Our house payment was fairly large for we bought our North Hollywood house when interest rates were double digit; we were paying somewhere around fifteen plus per cent. We also had our sports cars to pay for. We were nervous workers. It was very educational as well for Vera attempted to teach me the art of clean up, taking an animator's rough drawing and turning it into a finished work of art which would complete the movement of the animator's drawing. It was a great struggle for me. I never came close to being as good as Vera or as good as any of the clean up artists she worked with, but it developed in me a great appreciation for the talent of the clean up artist.

In 1985 Vera's dad wasn't listening to the real estate market for he wanted to retire and didn't want a mortgage payment to worry about. He couldn't foresee the explosion of property values at the time. He sold their house in Van Nuys and watched as the rents on apartments went up as well as the prices of houses. Before they sold their house Vera had offered to pay the mortgage for them but Vera's dad didn't think she would be able to do that because she was an artist and well, he didn't think an artist would make enough money to do that. We found a little house in Northridge near where they were living in an apartment. We put a down payment on it from the Porsche insurance money. When Vera owned her Porsche we drove it for fun, so it sat in the garage because we drove my car most of the time. I would kid her about selling it and investing the money. Was that an omen? Was the Master driver of the universe telling us something and I wasn't listening? Fortunately for us we could rent the house to them for a small monthly stipend of five hundred dollars and take advantage of the tax laws for second properties, it would be an investment for us and a home for them. The house was in a tract that had been part of a huge walnut orchard and it had four very large walnut trees surrounding it. The big trees framed the house and made it all the more inviting. It did need some work to make it livable: new floor coverings, walls moved so Vera's Italian mom had a bigger dining room for those delicious Italian dinners every Sunday, some paint and molding. It was all stuff Vera and I could do with the help of our friend, Don Klein. Our movie schedule at the time was not pressing so each evening we would leave work and go to Northridge to work on the house.

One evening after working on the house, we decided to have a late dinner before going home to our North Hollywood house. When we got home and entered our house we noticed the record turn table was running. Holes in our life quickly started appearing. The stereo was gone! The comforter on the sofa, the one my sister in law had knitted, was gone. In the bedroom we found an empty place on the dresser where Vera's gold plated antique Hungarian music box used to sit, a music box which played five Mozart tunes. And all of our jewelry was gone. My high school class ring, my antique pocket watch that Vera's dad had given me. All of Vera's jewelry gone and in the closet was a big space where Vera's silver fox fur coat used to hang; she'd given herself the coat as a gift and had her name embroidered inside. We were shattered. We felt our life had been severely violated because it was.

We had three cats at the time and one of them, Taco, was a very large savvy male. A few weeks before our house was broken into Taco had started acting strange. He behaved as if certain things were a threat to him. My shoes sitting in the corner, stuff like that. We even considered a cat psychiatrist because his strange behavior was becoming more prevalent. At the peak of Taco's strangeness our house was broken into. The cats all were very tense and skittish that night we came home and found we had been robbed. Taco was much more disturbed than our other two cats. We spent the rest of the night with the Los Angeles police doing the paperwork required for the police report. The police told us that the thief or thieves would be back in about thirty days. The thieves figure by that time you will have bought new stuff with your insurance money so they come back to steal new stuff.

We hurried and had a security system installed. It was exactly thirty one days later, a warm evening, about nine o'clock; music playing on the new stereo, Vera and I were relaxing after a day at work. Taco, who, after the robbery, had recovered from his strange behavior, started acting goofy again. Vera noticed him and said, "I'm going to set the alarm, Taco is acting nervous again." She set the alarm and as she turned to join me the alarm suddenly screamed out. We both turned to look at the key pad as she said "I just pressed the set button." I dashed to the back master bedroom and the alarm screen had been removed. I ran out to the backyard and the screen was on the ground. Vera and I had escaped confronting some whacko thief only because Taco, with that mysterious animal instinct, alerted us to the thieves for a second time. Earlier, days before the robbery had occurred, Taco was sensing something that caused his strange behavior. Odd behavior which got worse as the time for a robbery got closer, strange but true. Vera and I weren't listening and had no way of knowing what Taco was trying to tell us. We got past that flyin' chunk, finished fixing up the house in Northridge and moved Vera's folks in. They were happy for they thought since we were family, it was their house. The old folks were so sweet.

Vera's mom Josie, poor dear, she was a worrier. She was always worried that the house might blow down, blow up, blow over, or blow away. One day Vera and I went out to visit them and as we pulled up to the house it was just sitting there in the barren yard, all alone, not a tree in site. Josie had been so concerned that the wind would blow one of the big trees over and crush the house that she hired tree surgeons to sever each and every tree right off at the ground level. That is the closest I've ever come to a heart attack. Seeing that little house sitting there all alone without the trees and me, in my mind, subtracting the value of those trees from the value of the house sent me into a spiral of serious angst. My struggle to keep my emotions in check was considerable because the old folks had not mentioned to Vera or me the desire to eliminate about twenty five thousand dollars from the value of our property by cutting down the trees. But Josie wasn't thinking about property resale and I didn't have those warm fuzzy family feelings that obligated me to think that everything I owned was the communal property of the family. I was thinking of an investment for Vera that afforded her parents a nice tree-shaded place to live. But life went on and the house and the folks had to survive in the hot, west valley sun, without a speck of shade.

Back in Burbank there was a very important series of events occurring in the world of finance which was a world away from our problems at Don Bluth Productions and our house in Northridge. These events would have a drastic and lasting impact on the business of animation and ultimately a far-reaching effect on Vera and I. Roy Disney had resigned from the board of directors at the Walt Disney Company because of a conflict of interest. He owned a company called Shamrock Holdings that was run by a man named Stanley Gold. Gold was a shrewd investor who managed Roy's money very well. There was one investment that Shamrock Holdings owned that Gold said was unprofitable. Roy felt that it was because of the enormous amounts of money that the company managers had spent on real estate ventures and the neglect of the film division which was the heart of the company. Gold said that Roy should sell all of his stock and get out of the company completely or figure out a way to replace the management with one that would increase earnings. This became a very personal problem for Roy because this company was Walt Disney Productions, a company that had been started by his Uncle Walt and his father Roy O. Disney. Roy decided to see what he could do about turning the company around. He would have to raise many millions of dollars. He didn't have enough money to buy controlling interest in the company. To make matters worse there was a very rich man who had determined that the company that was selling for forty nine dollars a share was actually, if one sold off the pieces, strip off the assets, to use a financial term, would be worth one hundred dollars a share. He was going to pay ten dollars over the going price of the stock. To make a very long arduous story about high finance and court battles short, Roy and Stanley Gold found people to invest with him and they bought controlling interest in Walt Disney Productions. It was a long court battle but in the end Roy won. Over at the Disney studio Ron Miller and his management team were out and Disney Feature Animation was going to be saved. The mysterious money man who was going to save Don Bluth Productions had disappeared but in another world a chance for success was bubbling to a possible fruition. There appeared, from the background, another potential savior for Don Bluth Productions, Mister Steven Spielberg. Another chance for the phoenix to rise from the ashes, another chance to duck life's flyin' chunks.

CHAPTER 12
So We're off to Ireland

It was an important event for our studio when Steven Spielberg came to visit Don Bluth Productions in Studio City. He had screened *The Secret of NIMH* and liked it very much. He had a personal story he wanted to produce as an animated film and was visiting to discuss the possibility of Don Bluth Productions participating in a joint effort. The day of his visit he drove over to the studio in his Porsche. Don invited John, Gary and me to join him and Steven for an informal get together. Eventually the powers that be decided that Don Bluth Productions would do Steven's story as our next animated feature; it would be titled *An American Tail.* It was a story loosely based on the early history of the Spielberg ancestors but of course it would be told as a story about furry little animals. We all breathed a sigh of relief to have another picture to work on and were excited to be involved with a person as important in the movie world as Steven Spielberg and his animation company, Amblin Entertainment, with Universal Studios.

With a new production to work on, a move to a larger and cheaper space for Don Bluth Productions was in order. The guys found a nice building complex in Van Nuys, a couple of blocks from the Van Nuys airport. Compared to Studio City, with all of its restaurants and shops, our new home, our new neighborhood, was half industrial area and half private homes. One drawback for our new location, the area was free of Studio City type conveniences. There was one plus though, our new studio would be on Hart Street just a few blocks from The Airtel Plaza Hotel which was next to the Van Nuys Airport. The hotel had a very nice up scaled restaurant with a bar called *Landings.* I didn't know it at the time but later the bar became of great use for me and fellow worker, animator Dan Kuenster. After a long day working on *An American*

92

Tail we would take a break and spend a few minutes at the hotel bar to "down a couple of doubles", as Dan would say, and then head back to the studio to work late into the night.

Another blessing for our studio was a Mr. Morris Sullivan, a father figure with the wisdom of his years who came into the Don Bluth Production's fold when we were working in Studio City on *Dragon's Lair*, the video game.

A savvy semi-retired businessman, he wanted to get involved with animation as a legacy for his grand children. He had heard of Bluth's need for someone to help with the business side of things. A pleasant older fellow, always professional, he became a business consultant to Don Bluth Productions and Bluth Group Ltd. He managed and guided the companies through a bankruptcy battle with their game distributor. He even started a new company, Sullivan Studios, to employ all of us to produce *An American Tail* and *The Land Before Time*. Eventually, he had the company renamed Sullivan-Bluth Studio.

Mr. Morris Sullivan

In order to develop a future for us he began to investigate the idea of taking the company to an off-shore location. Eventually, he connected with the Irish government's Industrial Development Agency, the IDA, which is a government agency in charge of bringing new business to Ireland. They were convinced that to bring a prominent animation studio to Ireland would be an excellent new business for their country. Morris negotiated the deal, a contract, to bring key Bluth artists to Ireland with a Universal-financed film, *The Land Before Time*. As a preamble to the whole studio moving to Ireland, Morris worked out a deal with the IDA to hire one hundred Irish artists to be trained and to work in Ireland as cel painters on *An American Tail*. From that group, qualified artists would be chosen to move to California for training in other areas of animation and would help us finish *An American Tail*. There were twenty six, excited, young Irish artists who came to California to work with us. Sullivan-Studio set them up in the Oakwood Apartments on Sherman Way, a few blocks from the studio. With their European background and their excited energy, the Irish kids added a different spice to the stew of the studio mix and contributed their part to making what would be a fun film.

Our new studio in Van Nuys was a two story building. Vera and I had offices on the second floor in the front part of the building with large windows that gave us a view of the Hart Street neighborhood. She was on the west end as clean up supervisor and I was on the east side of the building with my effects department. While Vera and I were working hard on the picture the stresses of life caused our relationship to hit a marital speed bump; this slowed our frivolities considerably so we split up for a couple of months. It only took a two hundred and fifty dollar bouquet of roses the size of a Volkswagen Beetle, delivered to her room, to patch things up. Oh, the wonder of flowers.

On the morning of January 28, 1986, the Challenger Space Shuttle exploded about seventy one seconds into the launch. It was upsetting and everyone was slowed down by that awful event but we all recovered and continued our task of drawing a movie.

During this period a book came into my life which helped me through those downer events and became part of my mental foundation. It was a book titled *Creative Visualization.* When Vera and I were ironing out our differences we went to a counselor. On one visit, our only visit, there happened to be a book on a waiting room table which I picked up to peruse while waiting for the counselor. It was a philosophical book which I thought interesting so I made a mental note to get a copy for myself. A few weeks later when I arrived at work one morning I was very surprised to find a copy of that book on my desk. I checked with my fellow workers, asking who left the book on my desk, and Steve Moore, one of the effects animators in my department was the guilty party. Steve said, "I liked the book and thought you might enjoy it." I'm not a believer in the super natural but as I read the book I came upon a sentence that said, "If you're tuned into creatively visualizing your life, useful things will come to you, things like books." I still have trouble believing this story but I lived it, strange as it may seem. Studying that book and the gift of flowers worked much better than the counselor for that one single visit.

As we were finishing *An American Tail,* Morris signed the deal with the Irish Development Authority to move all of us to Ireland and set up the animation studio in Dublin.

1987, the Sullivan-Bluth Studio, the Van Nuys An American Tail crew

I wasn't too keen on the idea, I remember saying to Don Bluth, "Gees, Don, now we're gonna be immigrant animators?" I had a meeting with Don, John, and Gary and I told them I wanted $2,000 per week to go to Ireland. I wouldn't go for less. After much grunting and groaning, with Gary and John doing most of it, Don said "Okay, two thousand a week!" Vera and I sold stuff we didn't need, decided what to ship to Ireland, what stuff to put in storage and signed a deal with a company to manage our house in North Hollywood as a rental. We visited with a tax attorney to make sure it was true that we wouldn't have to pay income tax on the money we would earn in Europe.

A stress relieving Sullivan-Bluth Studio pool party at Gary's house

Too my surprise, one bright day, Gary appeared in my room and said they could only pay me $1,800 a week to work in Ireland. After some fuming and fussing, and Gary talking about how tough it would be to pay me what I wanted, I reluctantly agreed to go for the eighteen hundred a week. Considering the hassle of undoing all the preparations to go and knowing how disappointed Vera would be, I agreed to go. And it was only a two hundred dollar a week difference. It was more about the principle than the money.

While the plans for the move to Ireland were cooking, Sullivan-Bluth Studio hired several dozen California artists to help paint cels for *An American Tail* and had to lease the building across the street from our Hart Street studio to house them. We now had a very large number of people working for the studio in a neighborhood where the restaurant population was minimal. The Airtel Plaza had the classiest restaurant and was closer than the 94th Aero Squadron, a nice big restaurant designed to look like a World War II French farm house. It was next to the north end of the Van Nuys Airport runway so one could watch the aircraft take off and land while dining. Both of these restaurants were a bit too expensive for all of our struggling artists. Some Friday nights would find a few of us at the 94th Aero Squadron and some days a lunch at the Airtel Plaza but mostly it was fast food and long hours.

An American Tail was released November 21, 1986, and had a world wide gross reported to be $84 million. It was more successful than Disney's *Great Mouse Detective* which was released the second of July that year. Later, Bluth's *The Land Before Time*, with Spielberg's Amblin Entertainment, beat out Disney's *Oliver and Company* released at the same time. Don Bluth Productions had awakened Disney with three winning productions, *The Secret of NIMH, An American Tail,* and *The Land Before Time.* Disney had some work to do and later came out on top with a big hit, *The Little Mermaid,* which Vera and I were both privileged to work on.

In November of 1986, eighty seven of us, artists and technicians, plus spouses, children and pets began the move to Ireland. The IDA would pay the cost of bringing the Americans to Dublin and provide funds to train young Irish artists in the art of classical animation, provide equipment loans/grants, rent subsidies, and excellent corporate tax breaks. In return, Sullivan-Bluth agreed to set up a fully operational animation studio and the owners would live and work in Ireland for a minimum of ten years.

With our preparations for the move to Europe completed, Vera and I took off for Ireland during the early wintry days of December 1986. We flew into Dublin's air terminal on a dark, cold, wet, evening and met Gary and Kathy Goldman who drove us to a nice hotel in downtown Dublin. The hotel was classy Old World with lots of scrolly dark wood, very European. Rather formal but comfy. We stayed there the first few nights then moved into our townhouse which Kathy had rented for us in a Dublin neighborhood called Sandymount.

Our new home was a nice little, eight hundred square foot, townhouse with three bedrooms, and a small bathroom upstairs, and a living room, dining room, and kitchen, downstairs. It was in a new townhouse development called Lansdowne Village next to the soccer stadium and a stones throw from the Dublin Harbor which was the Irish Sea port for the city of Dublin. Although the town house was furnished there just weren't enough of us there, not very homey. But that changed when our personal belongings arrived from California. We had gotten used to the place sparsely furnished. We had a sense of freedom, you know, "freedom's just another word for nothing else to lose." So when the many boxes of our stuff arrived we were suddenly faced with what seemed like a huge task of sorting through it. Hanging pictures, storing video tapes, setting up the new television system that I had purchased so we could play U.S. videos as well as Irish videos, which were a different format called PAL. Rearranging the furniture, moving stuff upstairs, moving stuff downstairs, it was now more than luggage, we were now moving in for the long haul.

The Irish winter days provided only about six or seven hours of daylight. The sun came up about nine o'clock in the morning and set at about four o'clock in the afternoon and never got very high in the sky. Vera thought it would be a good idea if we had a tanning bed so we could keep our California skin color so on our next trip to London we bought a suntan bed. When it was delivered we squeezed it into the smallest bedroom upstairs. With the tanning bed against the wall there was only enough room for a small desk in the corner, where I did our international book keeping. Vera would be in the human toaster oven attempting to keep her California color from fading while I worked on the books.

The first several weeks we were in Ireland the building we were to work in wasn't quite ready. We spent our days running errands with Kathy, trying to learn the locations of stores and stuff and getting settled into our townhouse. Soon, enough of the new studio was finished so that we could go to work. We would have to start the early morning exodus from Sandymount, across Dublin to the studio. It would be very dark and very cold and sometimes raining when we left our warm little townhouse to head for work. It was very difficult to go out in the dark, freezing air. It always seemed so extra very dark in the mornings before the sun came up. I guess we were used to the bright San Fernando Valley street lights. No, it was that we were used to going to work after the sun had come up.

Our townhouse was just across the Dodder River and a few blocks from a DART station. DART was an acronym for Dublin Area Rapid Transit. It was a very efficient, Disneyland like, train system. To get to the station we walked up our short little street, past the old ivy covered brick buildings which housed a private girls' school, on across the Dodder River, dodging the seagulls looking for breakfast, on past the soccer stadium to the DART station to wait to be whisk to downtown Dublin, about five minutes away. We would take the train to Dublin center, get off the train and walk to a bus stop and wait at the dark, cold, usually wet bus stop to catch a bus to Phoenix Park. We never figured out which bus number was the correct one that would take us to the building that was becoming our new Irish studio.

Our building was on Conyngham Road, on the North bank of the Liffey River. We were across the road from Phoenix Park, at the time, the largest park in Europe. The river flows west to east through the center of Dublin, separating north Dublin from south Dublin before dumping into the Irish Sea at the Dublin Harbor. Each morning we would exit the DART, walk to the bus stop and wait in the cold. If we were lucky we would get the correct bus which would take us to the Sullivan-Bluth Studio. And if we were really lucky it wouldn't rain and we'd still be dry. Getting the right bus was a real struggle in the beginning for it seemed the Irish bus drivers like to put one over on the Americans by giving us the incorrect bus number for our destination. We would end up at a bus stop in a part of Dublin which we didn't recognize. It was always darkest before the dawn, as they say, so we would have to catch another bus and hope that we got the correct bus to take us to a warm, dry, brightly-lit studio, so much for public transportation.

After using that public transportation to get around and sometimes arriving at work looking like a couple of drowned rats, Vera was ready to head back to sunny southern California. For some silly reason we hadn't bought umbrellas and waiting in the rain for a bus just makes a person cold, wet and late. Later our discussion about going back to California ended with me saying, "No dear, we came to Ireland to do at least one film so we're stayin'." Of course I delivered a pep talk about staying just as she had delivered a pep talk about moving to Ireland in the first place. It was Vera that insisted on us moving to Ireland when the opportunity first arose. She was born in the San Fernando Valley at Saint Joseph's Hospital in Burbank, across the street from Walt Disney's studio. She had lived in the valley for what was her whole life up to that point. She wanted to see more of the world than the San Fernando Valley, Hawaii and the west coast of the United States. After checking with that tax attorney to make sure that we could work in Ireland without having to pay income tax I agreed to go. The U.S. had passed a law to encourage American company's working abroad to hire American workers with the enticement of not having to pay income tax on up to seventy thousand dollars of income. A lot of people don't realize how big their tax bill is because income tax is taken from you, a bit at a time, before you ever see it. It usually amounts to twenty five to thirty five dollars out of every one hundred dollars you make. That's a dinner out for every one hundred dollars you earn. So paying no income tax would be very good for us financially and not going to Ireland with Don Bluth Productions would have meant finding jobs in California which at that time could have been troublesome. Okay, it will be fun to go live in Ireland.

Vera and I decided we could survive the weather and inconveniences for at least a year so we arrived at a mutual agreement to stay in Ireland for a least one film. We decided that we would leave public transportation to those more in need of it and came to the conclusion that life in Ireland would be easier if we bought a car. After taking several used cars for test-drives we settled for a Nissan Mini, a very small sub compact which was only sold in Europe. The gender customs of Ireland kept Vera from being an active participant in the purchase. The salesman would only talk to me as if Vera was a non-person. The same thing happened when Vera went to the gas company in downtown Dublin to have the gas turned on at our townhouse. They didn't want to talk to her because she told them she was married. At that time in Ireland things like signing up for public utilities was a man's job. She went back later and talked to someone else and had success because she pretended to be single. At that time in Ireland wives seemed to be second class citizens. They paid a much higher income tax if they worked than did a working single girl. The Irish just wanted their wives to stay home.

I had become only slightly accustomed to driving on the left side of the street by test driving the cars which we were considering for purchase. The salesman would take me to Phoenix Park where the traffic was less threatening. There he would allow me to slip behind the wheel on what always seemed like the wrong side of the car. When I was a very young boy I wondered why a car's steering wheel wasn't in the center of the cockpit so that one would have a symmetrical view of the road ahead. It always bothered me that it wasn't. Driving on the "wrong" side of the road in Ireland convinced me of the correctness of my early idea. The steering wheel of an automobile should be in the middle. The real thrill was when it came time for Vera to learn to drive on the left side of the street with me in the passenger's seat. She eventually mastered it with only a few very scary close calls but after that I did most of the driving. Don't know why I didn't take her to Phoenix Park for that learning period. Instead I handed her the steering wheel to careen down what seemed like the wrong side of very busy streets with me helplessly sitting in the passenger's seat with no control except to excitedly wave my arms about and make loud grunts and yelps.

When we finally settled in our studio we started working on *The Land Before Time*, the original of course. Who would have thought that movie would generate so many video sequels in later years, thirteen at last count. Our building wasn't finished yet so there was much jack hammering and banging but we managed to get work done. Vera and I had decided that we had worked enough weekends and long hours on past films so we decided Ireland would be different. We would work a full day, no late nights, and take weekends off. We still got our work done and we managed to see some of Ireland. Well, I think we worked a couple of Saturdays and a few evenings.

I had an office on the third floor of the south west corner of the building. I was the supervisor of effects with a crew of about eleven artists working with me.

Ireland, with our special effects Land Before Time crew

In Ireland with Vera and her Land Before Time crew

I loved my second floor studio room there in Ireland. One whole side of my room had large windows with a view looking out across the Leffy River, across the railroad tracks, to the Irish countryside and the building in the distance which was the hospital where Oliver Cromwell patched up his British soldiers while he was murdering the Irish for personal gain. In the far distance were the Wicklow Mountains. To the left I could see beautiful sunsets painting downtown Dublin in shades of oranges and to the right was the bright green south western countryside. Not a bad view for the workaday world. And of course what Vera and I came to call the Irish lighting was always washing these views with splendid color and shadings. Vera was also on the second floor but on the east side of the building in a corner room with an even better view of down town Dublin. She was the supervisor of the clean up department and had about thirty five or forty artists under her command.

Vera had her cat Benji with her; he was a studio cat. She had acquired him when we worked in Van Nuys and she paid $1,500 to get him shipped to Ireland. Part of that expense was boarding him for six months quarantined in a kennel the other side of Dublin, out past the Dublin Airport. That was a fun drive for there were several highway "roundabouts" that I had to master but it was like a video game to make sure that after I round about-ed we were going in the correct direction. We would get up early each Saturday morning, have breakfast out, and then make the long drive out to the country to spend some time with Benji. Gary and Kathy would be there to see their dog, a German Sheppard they had brought over. Don would be there to visit with his company cat "Missy". Missy was such a part of the studio she was given a screen credit on *The Secret of NIMH*. Actually she was a very cranky, unfriendly, overweight, and most of the time nasty cat. She just didn't seem to appreciate a good home.

Weekends were fun for us. On sunny Sundays we would take long drives in our little car. We would visit small Irish villages and pubs, castles and ancient burial sites such as New Grange, a megalithic passage tomb built in 3200 B.C. We visited that site numerous times because it was a magical mystical place. As we explored the Irish countryside in our little Nissan we would play our collection of Hawaiian music on the car's cassette tape machine as we whizzed down the country lanes. At the time it never occurred to us to buy a condo in Hawaii after we were finished in Ireland.

During our weekend explorations, we would occasionally spot a castle or an ancient abbey which required further investigation. One Sunday we decided to visit a town which was on the map as a black period-sized dot. It was in the center of a vast peat bog in the middle of Ireland. We got there at dusk with a fog settling in and it so happened that there was no town. It was just a dot on the map with a name, they named a dot, a place where two, one-lane roads crossed in the middle of an enormous peat bog that went on as far as the eye could see. I stopped the car and got out to explore but Vera decided that she didn't want any part of the bog. She said it was getting dark and we had to go. Maybe she had read too many stories of finding dead people in the bogs whose skin had become leatherized. Vera was very careful about her skin. We left the peat bogs and arrived home safely after dark with our skin unleatherized and still sporting that nice tanning bed color.

On Easter Sunday, Ross Pollone, a friend and recording engineer with a recording date in London, came over to Ireland for a visit. We jumped in our tiny automobile and spent the day exposing our friend to Dublin and surroundings. It was getting on to late afternoon and we decided to tour Phoenix Park before heading back to our townhouse. It was a very big park with a lot of areas to get lost in and as we rounded a curve there was a young man lying by the road looking quite dead. We were trying to get the guy to respond when an older gentleman in a band leader's outfit came by. He helped us to phone for help and the ambulance guys arrived and carted off the half-dead lad. We never knew what caused his problem or what his final outcome was but the man that helped us, the band leader, was very appreciative of us Americans for he thought we had been very heroic in our efforts to save the formerly prostrate young man. He was so thankful that he invited us to his home for Easter dinner leftovers. It turned out that the family lived in the park and the man was the bandleader of the Phoenix Park Band so we accepted his invitation and went to visit with his family.

Now everyone lives their own life and this family was living theirs. The leftover food was piled on the kitchen counters and we were offered Irish coffee to chase away the evening chill. The mom fixed us ham sandwiches with the ham cut so as to have about an inch of white fat along one side. I'm not one to enjoy funny bits in the food I eat but I ate that sandwich like it was the greatest: thick buttered bread with mayonnaise and ham fat. We were super polite as Vera and I traded amused glances for such a different Easter. After dinning we chatted a bit and found out the family's son was an aspiring musician. When my friend Ross mentioned that he was a recording engineer a bond was formed and off we went with the twosome excitedly trading sound gear info. We thanked the family for their hospitality and the band leader couldn't praise us enough. He continued doing so as we said goodbye and moved out into the chilly night air leaving behind a warm Irish family.

On those rainy weekends we would usually stay home. Vera would watch her video of *Gone With the Wind* for the umpteenth time while I was in the kitchen making my favorite candy, chocolate peanut clusters. Vera cried every time she watched that movie, every single time, and I have yet to sit all the way through it.

While living in Ireland we did have the opportunity to travel to other foreign lands thanks to our friends Thad and Rachel, a married couple that worked in our accounting department. Thad was an experienced traveler with worldly experience. He liked to plan and take trips and had an unusually keen sense of where places were. We went to France and did the tourist things, visiting the top of the Eiffel Tower, The Louve, The Palace of Versailles, dining in marvelous French restaurants. We flew to Athens's with Thad and Rachel, where we boarded a cruise ship in the port city of Piraeus and sailed off to visit the Greek islands of Rhodes, Delos, Mykonos, and Santorini. On Mykonos we rented two motorcycles and with Rachel on the back of Thad's motorcycle and Vera hanging on to me we toured the island at speeds not safely conducive to good sightseeing. Back on the ship we dined and partied while we sailed up through the Bosphorus Straight to Istanbul where I learned that covered shopping malls were not an American invention. The Grand Bazaar of Istanbul dates back thousands of years and seems to cover many acres of land. We toured the Blue Mosque, St. Sophia, Tokapi Palace and numerous carpet and curio shops in and out of the Grand Bazaar. We spent a day at the ancient Roman city of Kushadasi and took a taxi thirty-five scary miles into the Turkish countryside to see the marble ruins of the ancient Roman city of Pergamum, which became the center of a large kingdom in the third century B.C. We visited the Roman city of Ephesus on the coast of Turkey and stood in an amphitheater constructed by the Emperor Tiberius Claudius.

Eventually the trip had to turn back to Ireland where Vera and I learned to escape harassment from Irish immigration authorities by walking through the gate that had a sign posted above it "Irish Enter." On an earlier trip, coming back form Paris, we had walked through the proper foreigners gate and had a heck of a time explaining to the guard, who, what, and why, we were coming into the country. Don't remember if we showed our passports, we must have. He was going to throw us out of the country until we explained our total situation and went over it several times. I never thought of dangling a twenty in his direction; that would probably have been jail time for sure.

We spent another great weekend in Scotland with our friends Thad and Rachel. They had shipped their nice, new, white Volkswagen Jetta over to use in Ireland and they drove it on our weekend jaunt to Scottland. We drove up to Belfast and boarded a ferry to Scotland. We visited Edinburgh, the town and the castle. We went to Inverness to see the Loch Ness monster, which was a no show. Surprise! We ended up coming back through Belfast in the middle of the night with the British soldiers, guns and all, running around our Volkswagen. The car almost stalled on the road up to the unlit border crossing where British soldiers we couldn't see in the dark were screaming at us to get across the border. It was a war zone. That trip had us arriving home so scared Vera went right upstairs and threw up.

Back to the peace of the studio, our movie, *The Land Before Time*, was progressing nicely. It was fun work but living in Ireland was a bit of a struggle for us spoiled Americans. The only evenings the grocery stores were open was on Thursday and Friday until nine o'clock. The rain was cold and plentiful and sometimes frozen. Yes, snow. We had several weeks of snow. It was a bad winter for Ireland. During this time the electric company went on strike so the city of Dublin would shut off the power in certain grids. This would cause havoc during rush hour for there would be areas where the stoplights wouldn't be working and there would be no one directing traffic. Apparently in Europe no one has ever heard of taking turns. When we approached an intersection the cross-traffic would just continue going through the intersection until a brave driver who wanted to cross the road would just have to push out into the traffic, laying on the horn, risking an accident. When that driver pushed a hole through the cross-traffic all the cars would then just continue in that direction until another brave soul made a dangerous effort to change the pattern.

When springtime arrived it was quite beautiful. The temperature was slowly climbing up the side of the thermometer and by June the days would almost reach seventy degrees. My friend, Joey Mildenberger, an effects animator, lived out on the Irish Sea in the village of Sutton. He lived in a nice apartment right on the beach and decided to throw a Forth of July party for the Americans. The day arrived and the sun was blazing. The temperature climbed to seventy five degrees. I thought it was going to be a great summer. Clear bright skies and warm sun-shiny days. We were ready for it. That day the local Irish inhabitants in their beautiful, delicate, mostly alabaster like skin, flocked to the beach, spreading out on their towels in the sun and plopping down for a good tanning. Vera said you could hear them sizzling on the beach "like bacon in a frying pan". On Monday many of out Irish artists were absent from work, home nursing their sun burns. I don't think the temperature was to reach seventy degrees again for the rest of that summer. It was nice though, for the sun was up at six o'clock in the morning and didn't set until around ten o'clock in the eventing. Nice, long summer days, just a bit cool, never hot, with occasional showers and still that spectacular Irish lighting.

For a break in our work schedule we would fly to London for a weekend of big city life. We would fly out on Friday night and get to London in time for a Mexican dinner at the Chi Chi's Bar and Restaurant, a big, two story, Mexican restaurant in Leicester Square. That restaurant was about as close to L.A. Mexican food as we could get while living in Ireland, which, at that time, didn't have a Mexican restaurant. Chi Chi's had good Mexican food, just like California and a yuppy style British crowd.

Don Hahn was living in London working as Associate Producer on the film, *Who Framed Roger Rabbit,* and we would occasionally have dinner with him when we visited London. He suggested that Vera and I were welcome to come to London and help on Roger Rabbit, the schedule was tight and character clean up and effects needed to be finished by the end of March. We had originally intended to work in Ireland to do two pictures in two years but we hadn't finished the first year. Our part of *The Land Before Time* was to be finished by the end of the year. Fortunately for Vera and me, Mr. Hahn was good enough to leave the offer open.

Morris Sullivan's office, on the third floor of the Sullivan-Bluth Studio, had been remodeled in the style of a formal English library, a perfectly appointed room with squares of dark wood paneling, framed with molding covering the walls and ceiling. One afternoon Gary Goldman stopped by my room and invited Vera and I up to Mr. Morris Sullivan's office on the third floor. Roy Disney and his wife Patty were visiting Sullivan-Bluth Studio. Morris, Don Bluth, Gary, John, Roy and Patty were already seated in the office when Vera and I arrived, and after hellos all around we stiffly sat down on a sofa to join the very interesting party. We had tea and crumpets and chatted mostly about nothing important. A relative of Patty's had been the ambassador to Ireland at one time and she told of staying in the Governors Mansion in Phoenix Park and how the butlers constantly tended the fireplace always making sure there was the fire going. We chatted and chatted and while I felt greatly honored to be there and was amused by the polite conversation, I kept wondering if there was something more important going on. It was a pleasant visit with nice, very rich people, but as far as I know there were no later negotiations to combine Sullivan-Bluth Studio with Disney.

Everyone was working hard on our movie when one afternoon I noticed a sign on Don's closed door, "Do Not Disturb, Door Will Open at 12 O'clock". So cold, unfriendly, un-family like. Don had started feeling the pressure of making an animated feature, running a studio, and planning ahead so there would be another picture for us to work on when *The Land Before Time* was finished. We were about half way through the year when I saw that sign on Don's door. I started thinking about what I would do if there wasn't a film to work on, if there was no work for me to do. I always liked our small, open-door, family-friendly, workshop studio. I always worked with my door open, closing it only for the most private and serious personal meetings with troubled artists.

This event initiated an ongoing discussion between me and Vera, a discussion about our future, about leaving Ireland when we finished the picture. We had planned on being there for at least two years or long enough to make two pictures and we were only about six months into our stay. Vera was reluctant to discuss leaving at this point for she had her department running well, we had a car, and she was comfy with all her girlfriends and Benji. She didn't want to leave them even though she liked the idea of moving back to sunny California, close to her folks, her sister Sara and Sara's three daughters. Of course, at this point we had no idea where we would work if we went back to California. Eventually, Vera and I decided we would move back to the U.S. after we finished the movie we were working on, *The Land Before Time* or "The Land Before Time Ran Out" as Vera called it. After Vera and I decided to leave Ireland we had several discussions about working in London on Roger Rabbit; Don Hahn was still open to the idea. Vera stomped her little foot and said, "I've had enough of Europe, I want to go back to California." I convinced her that another three months of tax-free income would be very good for us and besides, I said, "I agreed to come to Ireland for you so you need to come to London for us." I had gotten use to not paying income tax and it felt good. Finally she agreed to go to London. Dave Bossert, an effects animator working with me in Ireland, had already departed for London to work on *Who Framed Roger Rabbit* but I was always one to feel a professional obligation to finish a picture before parting with a company. Most everyone in the studio knew Vera and I had made the decision to leave the Sullivan-Bluth Studio when the film was finished. This was after we had crafted a letter of resignation and I had presented it to Don Bluth. "Are you going to get out of animation?" he asked. "No" I replied. "Animation is my life." There was no further discussion and as far as I know, no one at the studio knew we were going to work for Dan Hahn on *Who Framed Roger Rabbit* in London, but I'm sure it was an easy guess.

The goodbye party, Vera, Joey Mildenberger, and Anne Marie Bardwell

For sushi lovers there was only one Japanese restaurant in Dublin. It was very traditional Japanese and very good and we dined there often. One night our friends, Thad and Rachel, invited everyone from the studio for a surprise going away party for Vera and me.

It was an extraordinary party. The whole restaurant was reserved for our friends from the studio and we filled it to capacity, must have been a forty or fifty studio people.

More of our friends at the Dublin farewell party

Don Bluth, John and Gary couldn't make it, they had gone to Florida to record Burt Reynolds for the voice of a character in the upcoming production *All Dogs Go to Heaven*. Apparently Mr. Sullivan was assigned the job of wishing Vera and I well. The next week Morris, who also missed our farewell party, threw an official thank you party for us at the studio. It was an after work party with soft drinks and cookies. Vera and I were presented, as a thank you gift, several very nice, very large, pieces of Waterford Crystal.

With all of our hugs and kisses and good-byes finished we made our exit from Ireland. I was truly moved by Diann Landau as her good bye was delivered in a veil of tears. Shakespeare was right about a lot of things and "parting is such sweet sorrow" is certainly one of those things he was right about. I almost choked up myself.

It was a cold, dark morning when we left our townhouse. All of our belongings had been shipped ahead. We were excited for we were going to have a three week vacation in California before heading back to London. But there was a lot of Ireland we never got to visit; maybe someday I'll go back. The taxi arrived and we were off to the Dublin airport for the short hop to London. When we arrived in London we were to board a shuttle which would take us to the terminal where we would board our flight to L.A. As we approached the shuttle we saw Morris Sullivan being escorted by a very pretty young lady. They were headed for the same shuttle we were going to take to the aircraft. Apparently the lady was an escort provided by the airport to guide the rich and famous to their destinations. There we were, sitting on the same shuttle with Mr. Sullivan. After having said our good byes in Ireland it made for a bit of an awkward situation. It was like W.C. fields in the 1934 movie *It's a Gift*. He has his car packed with the family and their luggage, ready to depart for California. All the friends are on the sidewalk waving enthusiastically and yelling out their good byes as Mr. Bisonette, the Fields character, applies the gas to his engine only to have the car stall. Everyone on the sidewalk has expressed their determined good byes and the group is now standing there on the sidewalk, awkwardly fidgeting, quietly waiting for Mr. Bisonette to get out of the car and make an effort to start the engine with another vigorous cranking. When Vera and I saw Mr. Sullivan we were as the friends in the Fields film after having said good bye in Ireland. But I think we recovered the moment with friendly, humorous chit chat.

We parted company with Morris with a last good bye and boarded the aircraft. We went to coach and Morris went to first class. There is a lesson here but I'm not sure yet what it is. Years later I was invited to the fiftieth birthday party for John Pomeroy at a nice restaurant in Woodland Hills. John and Lorna had divorced years earlier and he was now married to Cami and it was Cami who had planned the party. Morris Sullivan was there; he had aged considerably and looked much older than I remembered him. He was in a wheelchair and was being attended to by a family member and didn't act as if he even remembered me. I felt sorry for the old guy. What good are fond memories of folks if you can't remember? No longer memories, no longer folks.

Vera and I suffered the long flight from London and arrived in Los Angeles for our three-week vacation. It was the end of 1987 and we were going to spend Christmas with Vera's family before heading back to London for our three month assignment. Vera's folks, Sam and Josie, and our cat, Taco, were very happy to see us and after our three week vacation passed they were sad to see us go. Taco sat and watched at the front door as we packed our luggage into the cab. Taco seemed very sad to see us go. I do believe animals can feel sad; this animal did. And away we went, headed for London to work on *Who Framed Roger Rabbit* for Don Hahn and three months of chilly London living.

CHAPTER 13

The Irish Lose Us to Merry Olde England

We arrived in London during a very chilly and sometimes very wet early January, 1988. Max Howard was the exceptionally friendly, efficient, and courteous British studio manager who welcomed us to The Forum, the building which housed our studio. The building was a nice three story building in Camden Town, a pretty area of London with lots of restaurants and good Greek food. Vera and I rented a three and a half story town-house apartment on Saint George's Terrace one street over from Regents Park and Primrose Hill. It was a brisk twenty minute walk to The Forum. The apartment wouldn't be ready for us when we started work so for our first week of work on the film we were housed in the Swiss Cottage Hotel, a very quaint, very British, hotel. Max was generous to supply us with a car and a driver to cart us back and forth to work for that week.

After we had moved into our apartment we no longer had a car and driver so we started walking to work. Primrose Hill Road ran along side St. George's Terrace and the two streets were separated by a tree lined parkway so we had a nice view of the park from the windows of our town-house. In the Disney animated movie, *101 Dalmatians,* Primrose Hill was where the dogs gathered for the "Twilight Bark" which was the signal to save the puppies. I worked on that film after I came back from my military service in 1960 and now Vera and I were living across the street from Primrose Hill. Our apartment was one in the row of fancy town-houses which had been built in the 1800's. Once a week the Queen's horses would be exercised and part of their trip was up Primrose Hill Road past our town house. There would be several dozens horses clattering up the street, quite impressive.

Each townhouse on St. George's Terrace was six stories high with what were once stables in the back and each had a basement where all the original kitchens were. Our apartment was the top three and a half floors with a laundry room and bathroom on the first level of the stairway. The living room was on the top floor with an expansive view of north London and a large sky light window on the other side of the room for southern lighting. From this room there was a short stairway that led up a half floor to an outside, sixth-floor, terrace which had a view across Regents Park and south London. From there we could see a Mary Poppins view of the chimneys on top of the townhouses, each townhouse sprouting its' own set. Of course none of the chimneys were functioning because they were remnants of the 1800's and now were no longer needed with the modern heating systems.

Our apartment was owned by a couple of young architects. They had remodeled this two-hundred-year-old home into a modern apartment with sconces of halogen lighting, fancy crown molding and high end Italian appliances. Below the living room was the kitchen and dining room and below that the master and guest bedrooms and baths. The master bedroom had large windows that looked out on Regents Park. All those stairs were a challenge after working a twelve hour day and walking twenty minutes each way to and from work but we did enjoy living there. Our townhouse was the second unit from the corner of Saint George's Terrace and next to us on the corner was The Queen Ann's Pub. On occasion we would stop in the pub for a pint to slack our thirst after a long day at the studio and the long walk home. The pub was usually inhabited by local neighborhood people who smoked cigarettes one after the other and owned dogs which they were allowed to bring into the pub. The cigarette smoke filled the room down to about shoulder level and the floor was knee deep in big dogs all laying around waiting for their masters to develop serious lung disease.

Each morning, at exactly ten minutes after six, rain or shine, we would meet Dave Bossert downstairs at the corner of Primrose Hill Road and Regents Park Road. Actually there was never any shine, it was too early for the sun to be up, very dark, but sometimes rain, a few times snow. Vera and I liked living on that corner; there were always those nice clean little London Metro cabs at our beck and call. We would use the cabs for social evenings but for work everyday it was expensive and we needed the exercise with the walk to work. Monday through Saturday, every morning, we would walk the twenty minutes it took to get to the studio. We would arrive at six thirty exactly. Dave had a key to the place so we would open the building for the rest of the crew who would began showing up from around nine o'clock onward.

Our London townhouse. Our entrance was to the left of
The Queens Pub in the sixth story building

The Europeans seemed to like starting late and ending not too late. We liked to start early and end early. We would work from six thirty in the morning until six thirty in the evening with one short hour for lunch, never longer. I was assigned a very small desk, with my back to the other artist in the room, in a very un-fengshie fashion. I was squeezed into a corner of a large room on the second floor with windows which opened the one whole side of the room to a view of East London. The first thing Dave and I would do upon entering the room in the morning would be to open all of the shades which covered the large windows so we could see the sun rise over London. As the rest of the crew begin filtering in they would pull down the shades and by mid morning all the shades would be down and the room would be a darkened tomb for the rest of the day with all of the British artists squinting into their glaring light boards.

It was a fun production directed by Robert Zemeckis with animation directed by Richard Williams. We all looked forward to the dailies which were very entertaining. The dailies gave me cause to think we were working on a film which had hit potential. If the dailies are entertaining, without color or sound, wouldn't the film have a good chance of being successful when it had color and sound? I thought so. To keep crew spirits up, Don Hahn, our associate producer, would make sure we had our Friday night get togethers, beer, wine, cheese and assorted treats. Those parties helped push us through those long weeks. Don always made sure we knew we had an impossible task ahead of us but he always reminded us that we were just the ones super human enough to do it. And we would do it. It felt good.

The first I had heard of the story *Who Framed Roger Rabbit* was when we were back in Van Nuys with Don Bluth Productions. We were nearing the finish of *An American Tail* and we were again on the verge of financial ruin. Don Bluth had been contacted by Steven Speilberg about directing the animation for a live action-animation film starring Roger Rabbit. There was good buzz in the studio for awhile. We were going to get hungry and we needed another picture to do. Working hard to finish *An American Tail* I didn't notice the buzz had stopped. One day I asked Don what had happened to Roger Rabbit. He said, "It's been shelved." End of story. I'm sure there were artist egos involved somewhere in that mix. But Vera and I ended up living in London, working on *Who Framed Roger Rabbit*

My animation on that picture consisted mostly of tones and shadows with a few "glints" or "sparkles" here and there. For most of the scenes I worked on, I would be handed a stack of registered photostats, black and white photographs of each frame of film. We would work over these photos and draw shadows and tones, tones being the shaded side of the character following the lighting of the live action shown on the photostat.

I did animate the train which roars through at the end of the picture after the dip machine has crashed through the back wall of the warehouse leaving a hole big enough for a train to drive through. If you stop-frame the sequence you can see in the train windows that mayhem was occurring on the train. In each of the train windows I drew silhouettes of people doing all sorts of things to each other, people attacking each other, native Americans in head-dress, Jessica Rabbit. I also animated the little railroad handcar with the pig operators that glides through after the train has passed. There was a sequence which I animated that didn't appear in the final cut of the film. It occurs over Toontown with a witch flying on a broom and Hercules in the sky throwing lightning bolts at her. Guess it didn't move the story. That sequence was cut out of the theatrical release but it did appear in a television release of the film.

After a few days of working on Roger Rabbit I went to meet the amazing Richard Williams. I had heard of him for years, who hadn't, and now I had the opportunity to meet him. He had a big office which immediately signaled his importance on the project as director of animation. I walked in and introduced myself and was instantly disarmed by his bowing to me. I was quite surprised. I should have been humbled in his presence but no, he bowed and said something about how amazing the heaving sea looked which I had designed and animated as the "Demon Wave" storm sequence in *The*

American Tail. I was quite flattered. Richard is a great fan of visual effects as his film *The Thief and the Cobbler* proved

He had spent his spare time working on that film for twenty-five years. One evening he invited me and Vera to see a couple of reels of the picture. It was visually spectacular. He was hoping Vera and I might find the time to help him and the other artist involved finish the picture. We never got around to helping and a few years later, because of some financial entanglements, he gave up the film to have it finished by Don Bluth et al. It came and went in the theaters. Disappeared with very little gasping but it has some remarkable animation, most of it on "ones", one drawing for every frame of film, for every character or special effect.

While living in London we spent a few of our Sundays sight seeing. And we had visitors from Ireland to entertain and of course we toured the famous art museums of London as well as the Natural History Museum and the British Museum. We went to Stonehenge on a very cold and windy day with our pals Thad and Rachel. We went to the city of Bath and toured the amazing Roman ruins under that city, which had been discovered in the 1960's when a farmer dug up a Roman helmet in his field. Bath was a city that the Romans took over in the first century. When we were there the spring water was still filling the baths that the Romans had built.

Near the end of production Peter Schneider's office called to ask Vera and me to meet with Peter during his next visit to London. Peter was the president of Walt Disney's Feature Animation. The day I met Peter he said, "Dorse, your reputation precedes you and it's a pleasure to meet you." I was very flattered. Vera and I had separate interviews with Peter and we were both excited to learn that he had offered each of us a job back in Burbank at Walt Disney Feature Animation. Peter asked me if I would supervise the effects department on the upcoming feature *Beauty and the Beast* and after that I would supervise the effects on some new sequences for a re-release of *Fantasia.* He wanted Vera to supervise the character clean up department for the pictures planned for the immediate future. We were very pleased to know we would have a job when we returned to California. I don't know who else Peter interviewed on that trip to London but I know there were people who had expected to be interviewed and were very seriously disturbed when he passed them by. It sounds maudlin to say, but Vera and I didn't realize that we had such a good reputation as the top people in our respective fields of animation. We probably have Don Bluth to thank for some of that, but then we hadn't given much thought to that and really didn't know how important we could be to Disney.

We finished our part of Roger Rabbit near the end of March, 1988, and had a wrap party in London. During this party all of the animators were ushered into a theater where producer Frank Marshall performed his magic act, a very entertaining performance. We had a birthday cake for Richard Williams, which Frank accidentally-on-purpose fell on, making a mess of it. Robert Watts, a co- producer of the movie with Frank Marshall, rehearsed all of the animators in an effort to sing the closing song of the movie, *Smile, Darn Ya, Smile*. The final take of that session was recorded and used as the singing voices of all the animated characters who sing at the close of the movie. It turned out quite well and we had much fun doing it. After the sing-along Don Hahn and Bob Zemeckis thanked all of us and shared their feelings about how wonderful we all were for working so hard on the picture and for doing such an amazing job. Don of course was very good as usual but when Mr. Zemeckis was giving his talk some of the British animators expressed, with rude sounds and gruff talk, their displeasure for being praised so highly knowing there would be no job for them after Roger Rabbit and Disney's exit from London. The moment put a slightly embarrassed cap on an otherwise wonderful evening.

After working twelve hour days, six days a week for three months, our work on *Who Framed Roger Rabbit* was completed. The artists did a remarkable job even though most of them who lived in Europe knew they would be finished with Disney and out of a job after the film was in the can. The studio had been very concerned about the movie's cost being somewhere in the $50 million range, and there was a time when the completion date looked as if it was impossible but the artists came through. With our part of Roger Rabbit finished, we hugged and kissed all of our London friends and bid them all sweet, tearful, sorrowful goodbyes. Back at our townhouse we packed our belongings, vacated our apartment, jumped in the waiting cab and took off for that long trip back to Los Angeles.

CHAPTER 14
Disney Wants Us Back

Home at last! We arrived in California the first of April 1988. We were going to start work at Disney Feature Animation in May so we had a few weeks to figure out what we were going to do about finding a house to live in. We sold our house in North Hollywood and were staying with Vera's parents in the house we were renting to them in Northridge. After searching for a few weeks we found a nice house for sale in Woodland Hills and bought it after our offer was accepted. It would be a long drive to the Disney studios but Vera wanted to be close to her parents just north across the valley. The house sat on the edge of a hill above Pierce College and had a 180 degree view of the San Fernando Valley from Chatsworth to Glendale. There was a nice, large, very private backyard, which looked out over the whole valley and a nice swimming pool to keep us cool during those hot west valley summers.

Because of the dinosaur connection with the *The Land Before Time,* it was a natural for Sullivan-Bluth Studio to have it's Los Angeles wrap party at the Los Angeles Museum of Natural History. Vera and I were invited and, of course, Don and John were there along with a great many other attendees. I didn't make an effort to approach Don; I wasn't sure how he would accept my presence. Thinking about it now and considering the museum environment it would have been fun if I would have approached Don, held out my hand and said, "Doctor Livingstone, I presume." I'm sure he would have enjoyed the moment. I did talk to a friendly John Pomeroy. He introduced me to Kathleen Kennedy, one of Steven Spielberg's producers for the film.

The Land Before Time was doing decent box office and Walt Disney Feature Animation was beginning to show signs of life after Roy Disney and the big money people had managed to gain control of the company.

Walt Disney Productions was restructured and renamed The Walt Disney Company and feature animation became Walt Disney Feature Animation. In 2007 the animation subsidiary was renamed Walt Disney Animation Studios. The downside for the animators, at the time, was that of all this positive excitement to expand the movie making side of the company meant that film production was going to need more office space for live action producers. In 1986 it was decided to move the whole animation department out of the famed animation building, which was on the main lot, to a building on Flower Street in Glendale. The effects department was pushed another notch down from that insecurity-producing, humiliating experience, by being placed in a pre-fab building in the parking lot across the street from the building that would house all of the other artists and administrators. That pre-fab building was where we did the effects for *The Little Mermaid* and where I finished the effects on the Roger Rabbit short, *Roller Coaster Rabbit*.

It had been nine years since Vera and I had resigned from Disney to join Don Bluth Productions. In May 1988, we had an appointment to meet with an administrator at the Flower Street building. We were to meet, separately, with Bill Dennis, the administrator who was in charge of contracts. Bill proposed salaries to both Vera and I which we did not contest. We were excited to get together after that meeting to compare notes. We were offered thirty five per cent less than we were being paid in London and we would have to pay income tax which was another thirty five per cent, so we actually took a seventy per cent pay cut. But we were glad to be back in California, just glad to have jobs and were ready to settle down. We didn't counter the offer.

The animation business was in a slump and Disney's animation department was just beginning to renew itself. Bill later told me that Vera and I were the first "big fish" that he, the administrator at the time, had landed. We didn't know the studio was attempting to hire everyone in the business that had animation expertise. I'm sure we could have held out for more money but we didn't want to haggle and we didn't have a clue as to how important they thought we were. We had been working in Europe for over a year and were out of touch with what was going on in the animation business back home. When I had my final contract meeting with Bill he offered me a $10,000 signing bonus. I was surprised. A bonus hadn't been mentioned in earlier conversations. I graciously accepted and signed a contract, feeling fortunate to have a job. The bonus was a nice plus. In fact the bonus made up for the few bucks that Gary decided they couldn't afford to pay me to go to Ireland. Sullivan-Bluth Studio gave me a nice increase in pay not too long after arriving in Ireland, and a per diem, so in the long run, with no income tax to pay, it all worked out rather well.

Disney hired Vera as a clean-up artist. She was disappointed that she didn't receive a signing bonus and we talked about it later. We thought that she should have asked for one. The studio apparently didn't appreciate Vera's reputation as the artist who had supervised the clean up department on three feature films, The *Secret of NIHM, An American Tail, The Land Before Time* and the first video games in history to use 2d cel animation. It took several years for the studio to appropriately reward Vera and the clean up artists for their hard work and talent. Vera's salary and bonuses then became very adequate.

Vera and I went to work on *The Little Mermaid* and each picture we worked on did better at the box office than the last. I worked on *The Little Mermaid* during the day and then in the evening I worked on *Oliver & Company*, directed by George Scribner. *Oliver & Company* was released before *The Little Mermaid* and with a fifty million dollar domestic gross it was successful enough to warrant a party. We had champagne and cake in the commissary of Walt Disney Imagineering across the street from the Glendale, Flower Street animation studio. Roy Disney was there along with Jeffrey Katzenberg and Peter Schneider. It was very special. A few weeks later the studio had a very big official wrap party for *Oliver & Company* in one of the sound stages on the studio lot. The decorating people had set up small restaurants around the inside perimeter of the sound stage and each restaurant featured food from a different culture, and of course there was music and dancing, always music and dancing. It was the biggest party I had ever been a part of. At that party Peter Schneider introduced me to Jeffrey Katzenberg and I was star struck. All of us who had worked on *Oliver & Company* received a bonus for the box office success; mine was $750. It was a beginning.

Peter and Jeffrey are super-smart and highly-motivated guys who helped put the Walt Disney Company back on top of the feature animated motion picture industry. Roy Disney took the job of steering the animation department and they were very anxious to have the best artists in the animation business working under their roof. Peter and Tom Schumacher, a producer and Peter's cohort, held several meetings with the key people in the animation department. With the Local 839 Union roster in hand we spent a couple of days discussing every name on that list. Each and everyone in the meeting who had anything to say about anybody on the list had an opportunity to speak. Another device the guys used to lure animation talent into the Disney fold was a bonus of $2,500 to anyone who referred an artist to the studio whose portfolio was accepted by the review board. The artist had to be hired and the bonus would be paid after that artist had been employed for ninety days. I got busy and filled out the required paperwork for at least a dozen good artists who I had worked with, but I an idea that would make the bonus referrals pay off really big! I would fill out the paperwork to refer everyone in the screen cartoonist union to the studio, but I was just too busy working on the movies to have time for that.

Who Framed Roger Rabbit was released on June 22, 1988, and was a big hit. The studio had a small wrap party for the L.A. crew. It was an outdoor party on the corner of Mickey Mouse Lane and Dopey Drive, the streets in front of the original animation building and the commissary on the main studio lot. Of course there was a band playing, always music and food, lots of food. At the Oscar ceremony in early 1989, Richard Williams won an Oscar for his animation direction on the movie. For the artist of the animation crew in California at the time. he had a small lunch party at The Carriage House Restaurant in Burbank to celebrate their work and his Oscar.

Richard celebrates his Oscar with some of the crew

To excite and inspire the artists about the Disney animation studio's future, Roy Disney planned a weekend retreat in Santa Barbara at a great hotel on the beautiful, peaceful, Pacific Ocean coast. Roy brought the key artists of feature animation together along with his wife Patty and the new president of feature animation, Peter Schneider. We all had beautiful rooms at the hotel and of course Vera and I, being married, were a package deal. The purpose of the weekend was no less than to discuss how we were going to continue creating successful animated films at Walt Disney Feature Animation, what it would take to regain the greatness of its past and to push it into the future. Vera and I were honored to participate in the discussions that weekend, it was an historical event. The Walt Disney Company and its animation division are forever woven into the fabric of that idea which is America. It was a great weekend and I was surprised on Saturday when Pat Riley, a famous professional basketball coach was introduced to the group. He had been invited to give an inspirational talk based on his success as a winning coach. I doubt if anyone remembers, but I had suggested inviting Pat Riley to the retreat to talk to our artists there. One day when Peter Schneider's secretary, Stacey, had come to my office to chat, we ended up talking about this important upcoming retreat and I suggested to Stacey that the artists, "being somewhat scarred by recent events, needed to have an inspirational pep talk." I couldn't remember the name of the coach of the winning Los Angeles Lakers basketball team, not being a basketball fan, but I thought he could give a talk that would be an inspiration to our artists. Stacey knew his name, "Pat Riley," she said. "I'll suggest it to Peter." That was the last I remembered of my suggestion until Pat Riley was introduced that day. I was proud and Pat Riley was very inspirational. At that retreat I also had the opportunity to thank Roy Disney for his enormous effort it took to save Walt Disney Productions from being taken over by outsiders. He replied "Well Dorse, it wasn't easy."

After the battle to save the company was won, Roy and Stanley Gold surrounded themselves with some very energetic and brilliant guys. They hired Michael Eisner away from Paramount Studios as Disney's CEO. Someone with Roy's people said, referring to Eisner, we need "a crazy like Walt," to head up the The Walt Disney Company, Eisner seemed to be full of crazy ideas. Along with Eisner came Frank Wells, a successful lawyer, to be President and business brain. Jeffrey Katzenberg, a very bright, long-time energetically driven co-hort of Eisner's at Paramount was hired as Chairman of Film Production and Peter Schneider was hired as the capable President of Feature Animation. Roy's efforts with Stanley Gold's financial genius had saved Walt Disney Productions. As a result the world has all of the wonderful animated films to enjoy from Walt Disney Feature Animation from 1984 to the present as well as all of the live action movies, theme parks and everything Disney. I didn't know at the time but my future had a light at the end of the tunnel.

This amazing story of Roy Disney with Stanley Gold saving The Walt Disney Company is told with great detail in the book *Storming the Magic Kingdom* by John Taylor. Roy autographed my copy. There is also a documentary called *Waking Sleeping Beauty* produced in 2009 by Peter Schneider and directed by Don Hahn. The film covers the studios great animated film success, 1984 through the super successful *Lion King,* an animation renaissance which occurred after Roy's successful recapture of the studio.

The Little Mermaid was a fun picture for me to work on. Vera worked in clean up as a Character Key and did a lot of the drawings of Ursula; I animated special effects. Mark Dindal was the effects supervisor. The herding of the artists in the department as well as making sure the effects animation was superb was on his shoulders. I came into the middle of the picture after having been in London when the production artists began working on it. There were no particularly damaging events to occur during the making of the picture and Mark did a good job bringing all of the effects together. We were working in the trailer in the parking lot and Mark would always have a health food sack lunch which he would eat at lunch time while he watched a soap opera on TV. He later directed *The Emperors New Groove* so I guess the soap opera's were research.

John Musker and Ron Clements were the driving force and co-directors behind the Disney version of *The Little Mermaid*. Mark and I would always show the scenes to John with the effects I had animated. I didn't know John until I returned to the studio in May of 1988. At the time, John seemed to be an adherent to the chain of command style of operating. When Mark and I would take our reel of scenes over to show John, I always felt John was talking to Mark, with me in the background. Mark was the supervisor so I understood John's respect for Mark's position, but when an idea is pushing on your grey matter and signaling your mouth nerves to start operating it can sometimes get embarrassing. On one of our visits, to show John some rough animated scenes, I felt confident about a solution to the problem in a scene we were studying. It was the scene in the laundry room where a laundress was using a period washboard. It is a very short scene, you would miss it if you blinked, but every scene in a movie, no matter how short, gets a microscopic evaluation. As the laundry lady scrubs a piece of material we see that Sebastian the lobster is caught up in the clothing and is being scrubbed like laundry. The scene wasn't working, it wasn't believable. As Mark and John discussed the problem I blurted out, "Guys, I know how to fix it, let me at it." I think I surprised John and Mark and their response was a positive okay. I readjusted the character timing and animated the cloth and the soap bubbles. The scene worked and John okayed it for the final reel.

During the production of *The little Mermaid* the studio announced that the artists would each receive a cel which was used in the production of the film. The studio had discovered that people were collecting cels as art and they were becoming valuable. When Vera and I went to pick up ours we were told that we must sign an agreement which stated that we would never put our cels up for sale. I thought that a bit strange, if I can't sell something I have, then I don't own it. We weren't being given a gift; the art was being loaned to us. So I told Vera that we should decline to accept the cel art and I would talk to Peter about it. When I met with Peter and told him the story he understood the problem. The agreement was changed so that if you accepted the cel you would promise to hold it for two years before attempting to sell it.

Ted Kiersey and I shared a room while working on *The Little Mermaid*; we put our desks back to back so we each had half the room. We had both taken an interest in learning to play cornets, a smaller version of the trumpet, and we each had acquired our own. We would practice on our breaks when there were no other people in the building who would complain. When Richard Williams came to L.A. for his *Roger Rabbit* Oscar he dropped in to visit me and to talk jazz. Richard was a horn blower from way back and trained with Max Kaminsky, a famous trumpet player who began life in 1908. Richard had a jazz band in London and would play Sunday brunches. How can one man have so much talent, time, and energy? When Vera and I lived in London Richard invited us to a hotel in Grosvenor Square for Sunday brunch and to hear his jazz band play. A curious moment occurred when the band started to play. I was going to video tape it, but the trombonist, a union man, told Richard that I would not be permitted to tape the performance. Wonder where that guy is now? Richard was okay with it but I was disappointed for his jazz band was very good and the atmosphere was very British. It would have been great to capture it on video, Richard Williams playing his horn with his jazz band.

Vera and I had, in the past, vacationed in Hawaii on several occasions and decided we loved the place. We needed to buy a condo there so we would have a place to get away from it all. We had settled into our Woodland Hills home and on our next break from work we headed to Hawaii. Vera and I had been to Maui and Oahu several times and I had lived on Oahu in 1959, but Kauai sounded more laid back and rural. A friend at the studio suggested we talk to some people he knew there and gave us names and numbers. He was a descendant of a family that were early missionary settlers who came to the islands to save the souls of the natives and ended up owning a lot of their land, funny how that works.

We flew over to Kauai with a video camera stuffed in our luggage, found a condo to rent, our home for two weeks, met our youthful, sweet, real estate lady, Linda, and spent a week video taping condos. Each evening we would go back to the nice condo we were renting and settle down to view the tapes I had made that day. After a week of viewing tapes we made a choice, condo 521 in the Nihi Kai Villas at Poipu Beach, Kauai.

Nihi Kai Villas

That was the sunnier, dryer south side of the island. It's a very short walk from the Nihi Kai Villas to Boogie Board Beach and a bit farther up the beach is Poipu Beach Park and Bennecke's Beach Broiler where you dine upstairs with a view out over the park to the ocean. Our condo was up across the road from the ocean close enough to see the spinner dolphins jumping out of the blue Pacific.

In October 1988, after deciding on which condo to buy, we spent the next week dealing with the legal stuff required for our condo purchase. We said good bye to our new-found island friends and our new home away from home and flew back to California feeling good about having a home in Hawaii to run off to between breaks in our movie schedule.

Soon after arriving back home from Hawaii the studio had a wrap party for *The Little Mermaid* crew. The party was held in The Beverly Hills Hotel. I still remember the long line of automobiles crawling into the parking facility. It was a formal affair and it was the first time I wore my snake skin cowboy boots with my tuxedo. Of course, with the boots, I towered over Vera who was, or is, five foot three. She wore a formal backless dress which was very stylish but her cleavage was bringing up the rear. A more beautiful plumber's crack has never been exposed. Though the party room was small and the food fairly sparse, compared to the *Oliver* party, the party was more formal and I felt it rightfully honored the artists who had worked so hard to make the movie a success, after all it was The Beverly Hills Hotel. I do remember having a discussion with one of the young character animators there at the party. He had already carved out a very strong reputation for himself as a character animator. He was from Europe and was thinking about returning there. I thought that would be a risk to his career since his star was just beginning to shine at the studio. I made a hearty attempt to convince him to stay in the U.S. He's still here and one of the most talented animators in the business. I wonder if I was really effective in our conversation or if my memory just drags my ego up for a good polishing.

Some time after finishing *The Little Mermaid,* the studio ask me and Ed Gombert, a talented Disney story guy, to go to a film festival in Varna, Bulgaria, which was to be held in October of 1989. I thought the trip would be interesting if not scary, having never been in a communist-run country. The studio gave Ed and me each $1,400 and an airline ticket for Plovdiv, Bulgaria with a short stop-over in Paris. I didn't know landing in Plovdiv would require a long bus ride to get to Varna. Why didn't we just fly to Varna, it has an airport?

I was never quite clear as to our duty on that trip but I think we were basically representing The Walt Disney Company and were to be intelligent American film people. We landed in Paris and spent the day waiting for the evening flight to Plovdiv, Bulgaria. We were to meet other festival people there and then be bussed to Varna. Ed and I, silly Americans, approached the information desk at the Paris airport. It was occupied by a pretty French girl whom we attempted to communicate with by speaking way too loud, separating syllables and enunciating like ignorant foreigners. She spoke perfect English as she directed us downstairs where we were to talk to a Bulgarian official. We found our man, crouched behind a desk, looking like a wanted mafia figure. He spoke English, was very polite and we had no trouble following his directions to the waiting area for a flight to Plovdiv. It was late afternoon when we boarded a Russian-made Tupulov 134. It was a design similar to the Boeing 727 but the interior reminded me of a 1940's camping vehicle, wood paneling with curtains on the windows. After we were seated Ed reached up to pull the curtains open and something fell off the wall. All of the other passengers, people from several countries, roared with laughter when the piece, whatever it was, hit the floor with a bang and rattled to a stop somewhere under a seat. Ed was never a brave flyer so it un-nerved him a bit and caused me to wonder why the raucous laughter which I thought puzzling. We buckled up and taxied out to the runway and I think I might have prayed for the plane to get off the ground. We did and it was a beautiful sunset flight over the Alps and the Matterhorn.

We landed at a small airport in a rural area outside the town of Krumovo, Bulgaria which appeared to be a suburb of Plovdiv. It was a small airport and after a ground crew wheeled a portable stairs up to the plane we exited the aircraft. We had to walk a short distance to the airport building and were met by a young Bulgarian security man, guns and all. He inspected Ed's bags but didn't bother with me, I wondered, do I look Bulgarian? The airport was a tiny place and as we passed through a double door to the outside there was a group of taxi drivers trying to acquire their last trip of the night. They were yelling at us for a fare and I tried to explain that we were there to meet a lady from Sofia. With that they all started yelling, "You want lady, we get you lady." Finally we convinced them that we wanted a taxi, not a lady, so we chose one of the more reserved drivers who spoke English. We told him we needed a nice hotel and he immediately asked if we would sell him U.S. dollars. He knew of a nice hotel in town and proceeded to drive us there all the while injecting the conversation with a plea for U.S. dollars. I wasn't about to end up in a Bulgarian jail so we kept refusing his pleas but made it clear that we needed for him to pick us up at nine o'clock the next morning. I don't remember much of our stay at that hotel. I was exhausted, the dinner good, the room restful and the Bulgarian breakfast made our stay feel almost like home.

I was very relieved the next morning to see our cab there at precisely nine o'clock. We arrived at the airport terminal without submitting to the cabbies demands for dollars and in the daylight we could see the main terminal was about the size of my house. The interior had marble floors that looked like they had not been mopped and polished since the Roman days. We didn't see a soul that looked like a film festival person so we sat down to begin a long wait. There were people coming and going. There was a booth in the corner selling dried cheese sandwiches and some kind of watery juice drink. Fortunately we'd had a nice, capitalistic type, Bulgarian breakfast before we left the hotel that morning.

After waiting and wondering all day some festival folks showed up at about ten o'clock that night. Most of them were film makers from different countries around Europe and a few from the U.S. None seemed impressed that Ed and I worked for Walt Disney. It was no doubt, artist's egos at work. After introductions all around we boarded a large bus and after a couple of wrong turns and a stop for directions we were headed for the Black Sea where the city of Varna clung to the coast.

The Trip: It was a very dark, moonless night. A lone bus was struggling along the narrow, winding, forest-lined, and mountainous road. The driver, a burly, sweaty Bulgarian, gripped the steering wheel tightly as he anxiously looked for some sign that we were on the right road. I was crumpled up in the very narrow bus seat bouncing like a pile of dirty laundry, tumbling in and out of sleep. In a semi wakeful moment I tried to find the glowing face of my Swiss Army watch to confirm my suspicions. After a struggle in the darkness I finally focused in on my watch. It was true! I had been on this bus, in the middle of a communist Bulgaria, bumping along a dark mountain road since the beginning of time. I was in Bulgarian Bus Hell.

Finally the bus pulled in behind an old building in some little village and the driver announced it was a rest stop. We all dismounted the bus to find a little restaurant in the back of the building. As we entered the restaurant, a nice cozy place, we scanned a series of tables mostly occupied by young Bulgarian soldiers. Why they were there we'll never know but they seemed to be having a good time. I had learned that in unrestricted countries where Westerners traveled the local people spoke English: it was good for business. In countries such as the eastern communist countries like Bulgaria, very few people spoke English, which was the case in this little tavern but we made do, pointing at the bread and drinks we desired.

The entertainment for the evening was a trio of gentlemen dressed as cowboys. Not the rugged western American cowboy but dressed kind of like if Groucho Marks dressed as a cowboy. The oddest part was that the lead singer of the group did Louie Prima. All of the songs he sang were Louie Prima's songs sounding just like Louie Prima. Of course I've always liked Louie Prima and in the middle of the night, in the middle of Bulgaria, a guy dressed like a comedy cowboy doing Louie Prima was worth the trip. As we finished our break and all headed for the door the lead singer cowboy embraced us Americans and told each of us how much he liked Americans. Of course his English wasn't designed for my ears and I couldn't speak Bulgarian but he was smiling so I felt reassured. The soldiers never seemed interested in us so we all got back on the bus and away we went.

We arrived in Varna in the morning at about three o'clock and were greeted by the lady appointed as our liaison. As we all checked into the hotel I told the desk clerk at the counter, who spoke English, that I wanted a room no higher than the third floor. Not only do heights bother me but at the third floor there are just two floors of people smoking in bed below. For some reason I think two floors of smokers are better than six or twelve. We got rooms on the sixth floor. The desk clerk explained to us that the first three floors were offices. We boarded the elevator and pushed the button for the sixth floor. The door was one of those open gates that closed and allowed us to watch the hotel innards scarily fly by as we rose to the sixth floor.

Ed and I felt as if we were the only people on that floor so we unpacked our flashlights to explore. The third floor was dark as we checked the stairwells, stored full of furniture. The door to my room looked like it had been kicked in and the carpet on the floor was wrinkled. The next day I tracked down our "Lady for Keeping Us Happy" and told her that we needed a better hotel. She said there was one a bit out of town, we'd have to taxi in, and it would cost us money because the first hotel was part of the Disney program so it was paid for. Ed and I asked her to show us the other hotel and eventually we ended up in a slightly nicer hotel a taxi ride away. It had a restaurant with food that was very much like good home cooking. One evening we dined there with two couples

Me under the arch at the Roman spa

from East Germany, that conversation went no where; serious language barrier. We had another evening of dining when the Film Festival people brought together a bunch of us folks. We sat at a table with several Cubans who spoke as much English as the German's did, that conversation also went nowhere. It's embarrassing and uncomfortable to be unable to speak another's language. The story of God causing the people to speak different languages so they couldn't communicate well enough to build the tower of Babel, a building high enough to get to heaven, sure worked. I found it hell trying to communicate without a common language and was sure we'd never get to Heaven that way.

Each day, after breakfast, we would retire to the theater. We spent nine days watching many films from the eastern bloc countries. Films with dreary stories of endless efforts to accomplish something only to have the effort end in failure. It was enough to put a person to sleep. Ed and I did get a lot of sleep on that trip.

The festival finally came to a close but not before Ed and I had a chance to explore the local museum, amazing gold sculpture collection, and the Roman ruins in the middle of the city. The Romans had built a health resort there but it had been covered over by the city that grew over it. Don't know how that works.

The Bulgarians had passed down the story of the lone tower that stuck out of the ground and called it the Roman Tower but nobody knew for sure what it was until archaeologists dug into the ground and excavated a whole Roman health fitness center, covering several acres, which even had a wood-burning furnace to heat the water in the facility.

With the film festival over Ed and I vacated our hotel and jumped in the Mercedes sent to pick us up, it was late, making Ed and I very nervous. We had a perilous drive to

Ed celebrating his existence on a Black Sea beach at Varna

126

the airport on the other side of Varna where we boarded a small Russian prop job with wrinkled carpeting in the cabin, just like my hotel room. Away we flew to Munich, Germany to board a very clean, tidy, German Lufthansa jet. Then on to London where the security was frightening but we finally got through and arrived at the aircraft which would take us to Los Angeles. Other than having oil stains on the engines and some of the Velcro fasteners on the seats loose, we were happy to be aboard the aircraft even though we had to sit there for more than an hour because of heavy traffic over Scotland. I thought I would never get home. We had finished our movie *The Little Mermaid* before Ed and I departed for Bulgaria and when we finally saw the aircraft that was flying us back to L.A. we were amused to see the name painted on the side of the 747. In big script letters was the name The Mermaid Clipper.

After arriving home from Bulgaria I was assigned to a featurett called *The Prince and the Pauper*, starring Mickey Mouse and directed by George Scribner. That was a short assignment which kept me busy until we started on *Beauty and the Beast*.

Our future looked very bright: *The Little Mermaid* was a big hit with its domestic gross over $84 million and we owned the cels we were given. Every one was happy.

CHAPTER 15

The 2ᴺᵈ Golden Age of Animation Blooms

During our slow time, before we were into the heavy lifting on *Beauty and the Beast,* we had another retreat. This one was held on the RMS Queen Mary, which was anchored and welded to the harbor in San Pedro, California. We all had rooms reserved for us on the ship so we could be around for the evening's dinners and festivities. The leading members of the animation crew were there as well as Roy and Patty Disney, Peter Schneider and Max Howard. Max came to the U.S. from Britain after Roger Rabbit was finished. He was brought over to manage the Florida animation studio and now was in California managing the Burbank studio. Vera and I were looking forward to spending a couple of nights on the ship. We dismissed the stories of the ship being haunted but the stateroom we had was from a comfy luxurious past which could have inspired a ghost or two.

The first evening we were there we all met for dinner at a nice restaurant across the bay. Peter had invited a man to give a talk after dinner about *The Little Mermaid* story. It was an interesting talk but it slanted too far toward sexual implications of the story, if anyone could believe those implications were actually there. Afterward we all joined for drinks in the aft bar of the Queen Mary and from what I gathered, Roy was none too pleased by the talk of a Disney film with an underlying story line which was pointing over to the side which we don't talk about. But we had a good time.

The Walt Disney Company owned the Queen Mary and the next day as we were having our all day long meeting in a huge room, somewhere in the ship a band, which we could hear, was rehearsing. Some one had to go tell the

128

band that they were disturbing our meeting and the owner of the ship, Mr. Disney, was on board and they would have to rehearse somewhere else. And that was that. For some reason, I think the meeting the next day ended early and I'm not sure why. I didn't feel as if we had accomplished what we set out to do but for Vera and me it was a great weekend.

I began work on *Beauty and the Beast* and Vera began working on *The Rescuers Down Under,* which was being produced by Thomas Schumacher as a sequel to the original *Rescuers.* Vera was to be assigned, she thought, to supervise the clean up department. I was told that the animators on that picture each wanted to choose their own clean up artist and not have a clean up department. Vera had not been consulted about this method of dealing with clean up. She had supervised the clean up on several movies and knew how it needed to be done to insure the meeting of the deadlines with artful animation. She was very hurt to be bypassed so immediately.

We always drove to work together and Woodland Hills, where we lived, was a long drive on the crowded Ventura Freeway. The driving time on the way to and from work gave us many hours of discussion trying to figure out a way to get past Vera's hurt and the studio's seemingly total disregard of her history and success. Vera resigned herself to go with the process but after awhile, I think it was a couple months, the clean up department was failing to achieve its goals and it took no great vision to see that the picture would not be finished before the budget was used up. When a movie, which is never an ensured success, costs many millions of dollars and starts to go over budget by hundreds of thousands of dollars a week, with hundreds of people getting weekly paychecks, the accountants start grabbing their chests and collapsing in the hallways and the clutter makes the movie even harder to finish. The method which the clean up department decided to use, each animator with his own clean up department so to speak, was not working. The system was revised and Vera was assigned to be a Supervising Character Lead in the clean up department but according to the film's credit list there were five of them so Vera was never put in charge of the whole department, much to her dismay. I must say that I only heard Vera's side of this story but I lived with her pain so I have no reason to doubt it. The film was completed but unfortunately a picture can be completed within a budget but it still has to make money and *The Rescuers Down Under* didn't make enough.

On *Beauty and the Beast* there was a clean up crew assigned to each of the cartoon characters and each crew was headed by a key clean up artist. When Vera finished with *The Rescuers Down Under* she was assigned as the clean up supervisor over all of the key cleanup artists working on *Beauty and the Beast.* Our drive to and from work became much more recreational and pleasant after she accepted that assignment.

One day Vera brought home a little orange kitty. She hadn't discussed orange kitties with me, or any other color of a kitty for she knew that sight unseen, I would reject the kitty idea. It's awfully hard to reject a kitty when it's right there with those big kitty eyes looking up at you wishing for a life, so we had *Beatle* or *Beetle*; Vera named him but we never wrote the name down so spelling doesn't matter. These were okay pet days at the studio for Peter Schneider allowed people to have their pets at work. I don't think he allowed it so much as he just never said people couldn't, so people started bringing their pets in and kept them in their rooms as they worked. So Beatle learned to ride to work with us. He would lie down on the top of the dash of Vera's van and away we would go down the Ventura Freeway. Beatle seemed content to squeeze against the windshield, occasionally snoozing and watching the movement of all the cars in the stop-and-go traffic. Vera had a litter box in her room at work and Beatle never strayed out of the room. As people who had business with Vera visited they would always take the time to caress Beatle and he loved the attention.

Soon the pet thing became a problem. Debbie brought in her snake. Kathie had rats in the background department where she had a big panel at her door making sure the rats stayed in the room. Umm, snakes do eat rats. I don't remember any birds but there were dogs of several sorts. After awhile the menagerie became a problem for some people so the question came up with the review board which was composed of artists who were key animators and supervisors. At these meetings we would discuss business and review portfolios of artists looking for a job at the studio. As a group we would decide if an artist was employable but that day it was the pet thing we were discussing. Most of the people at the meeting agreed with no pets at the studio so Peter announced that there would be no more pets, creatures, or animals brought to work, case dismissed. So Beatle had to stay home after that. By this time he was a good size tom cat and a very lovable creature. Vera and I hated to leave him at home by himself while we were spending those long days at the studio drawing movies but Beatle did survive that lonely experience, of course, he was a cat, a very smart cat.

The beginning of *Beauty and the Beast* was a bumpy one. When I interviewed with Peter Schneider in London he had presented me with the opportunity to supervise the special effects on *Beauty and the Beast* and *Fantasia/2000*. I was excited about my future and was to have my first meeting with the producer of *Beauty and the Beast*, Don Hahn. I had known Don since the early 1970's and we had worked together in London. Our chat about the production started as a friendly, casual chat but quickly, for me, turned sour when Don, in the course of the conversation said, "Gary and Kirk wanted Mark Dindal to supervise the effects but he doesn't want to do it." Gary and

Kirk were going to direct the movie and I totally overreacted and felt the job would be hard enough even if the directors loved me like their own child.

I was already experiencing resistance to my leadership with people in the department who had developed strange animosities toward me or anyone who had worked with Don Bluth. It was a very odd time for me and of course there were, I guess as in almost every department anywhere, people inclined to play the political game. I think sometimes that comes from a lack of confidence of their own basic abilities and results in a need to manipulate a situation by maneuvering in the shadows and spewing negative colorations of the more successful fellow workers. This strange animosity could have been bred by the history beginning in the early 1980's. At that time Walt Disney Productions animation film production was floundering, the whole company was about to be gobbled up by investors and sold off in pieces. The animation department was working on *The Black Caldron* which ended up as the most expensive Disney feature to that date and a box office failure.

Don Bluth was making successful animated films; Don's film, *The Secret of NIMH* released in 1982, helped turn around the animated feature film business. Steven Spielberg's interest in *The Secret of NIMH* brought him into the Bluth realm and the next two pictures Don Bluth Productions did with Amblin Entertainment, *An American Tail* and *Land Before Time* were more successful than Disney's two releases at that time, *The Great Mouse Detective* and *Oliver & Friends*. Steven Spielberg and Don Bluth gave Disney's a kick in the pants with successful animated features. If things had gone just a little bit differently, those people who were critical of Don Bluth Productions would not have had a future at Disney, for there would be no Disney.

Back to my *Beauty and the Beast* meeting with Don Hahn, I blurted out, "I don't want to work with directors who want someone else to head up the effects department; sounds like they don't want me." Looking back now I see that it was very arrogant and shallow on my part. I've always been too reactive, I'm still working on that but then it was too late. I played the wrong hand and Don, seeming surprised said, "We have to go talk to Peter." Well that meeting with Peter Schneider was no fun. At the meeting with Peter I said I thought I had been downgraded and he said he wanted me to head the effects department. I asked him, "What if Mark had taken the job" to which Peter replied, "He didn't take the job!" This went on for awhile until I said that I didn't want to head up the effects department. The meeting ended on a "well that's done" note as if the issue was settled but I was still very rattled by the whole experience. That next Monday morning Peter and Bill Dennis arrived at my room, minutes after I did, to see if I would change my mind. They finally talked me into working with Gary and Kirk so I was now caught up in the frenzy of starting a very important movie. I had lunch with them and all was very cordial between us. I'm sure they wanted Mark to head up the effects department simply because they knew Mark and felt more secure with Mark, and then again maybe they thought Mark was just a better effects artist and department head than I.

I received a pay increase of fifteen per cent on my salary and stepped, head first, into the wind storm of excited artists, determined managers, and political adversaries. It was no fun. Working with Bluth all those years allowed me to have a generally good-spirited, talented, crew of artists with minimal politics and maximum effort. There were very few people between me and my effects work which made it to the screen, mostly just Don Bluth. Now I felt that not only did I have the picture to work on, I had a few guerrilla fighters and politicos demanding my energy. It just wasn't fun anymore and I finally declined to continue as supervisor of effects. I still regret that I let the more political people in my department win, those who seemed to have an ax to grind rather than a film to make. Peter let me keep my salary increase and Randy Fulmer became the effects supervisor on the picture. Of course the politics continued but the negative energy in the department was directed at a few of the other young artists whose talents the politico's were jealous of and threatened by. Randy took on the task of supervising the department and succeeded in completing a very difficult task and lived to tell about it.

Occasionally the studio would have a luncheon to honor a person who had been given the title of Disney Legend. Their name and hand prints would be imprinted in a bronze plaque and installed in the pavilion area fronting the team building, the building with the statues of the Seven Dwarfs holding up the roof. Vera found out that the next luncheon was to honor Sterling Holloway; He was an early movie star whose career had started in the 1920's and Walt Disney had used his voice in many of the early animated films. She knew that he was related to a cousin of hers and so she used that connection to get us invited to his luncheon. There were only about a dozen people there so it was a fairly exclusive group.

The luncheons were held in a dining room in the studio commissary building so the day it was to occur I made sure I was there early. Michael Eisner and Roy Disney were standing at the commissary patio entrance when I arrived so I walked up to them to say hi. I had met Eisner a few years earlier when he was President of Paramount Studios. My girlfriend at the time was his secretary and one evening I went to Paramount after work to pick her up for a date. When I went up to the President's office she answered my knock and was eager to show me Michael Eisner's office. He was out of the office so she gave me the grand tour. The office was larger than the house I'm living in now with everything you would expect a Paramount Studio's President's office to be furnished with. Just as we were leaving, Mr. Eisner and another gentleman entered the office. I don't remember being introduced to the other gentleman but I think it was Jeffery Katzenberg; Eisner and Katzenberg were very close working partners at that time and Michael is very tall and Jeffery isn't, as it was with the two men standing before me.

During my visit, there at the Disney commissary with Roy and Michael, I told Michael that story about my girlfriend as his secretary. His immediate response was a quick "Well, did you marry her?" To which I said, "No I married a girl I met here at the studio." And just about that time, Vera walked up and of course gave Roy a hello kiss. After Michael said hi to Vera he turned to Roy and suggested that the company run a story in the Disney Newsreel, the studio paper, asking for people who had met at the studio and married to send in a picture and a paragraph. Their story would be published in the paper. Several months later the article appeared in the paper requesting submissions. I got busy and wrote a paragraph which I submitted with a picture of me and Vera. It was later published in the company paper, The Disney Newsreel, February 14, 1992, along with several other couples' entries, thanks to that meeting with Roy and Michael. It's amazing how two super wealthy, powerful, busy men can be concerned with such a simple idea and make it happen. It was probably only a phone call one of them had to make but one of them remembered and made it happen.

While working on *Beauty and the Beast* Vera and I spent the year remodeling our house in Woodland Hills, making it about thirty per cent larger. During that remodel we had a severe rain storm while the whole back of our house had been opened and covered only with plastic sheets. The water started running in under the plastic and as it snaked across the floor it threatened our furniture, sound system and TV. Vera and I worked all night using all of our blankets to dam the water. Vera had the great idea of using the washing machine to spin the water out of the blankets. The dryer isn't designed to sling the water out of blankets so we were working like beavers, spinning the water out of the blankets in the washer and replacing blankets at our dam where the water was coming in. At about five o'clock in the morning we both collapsed and fell asleep in chairs in the room. We awoke a couple hours later and the water hadn't damaged anything yet but it was still raining. I hurried to the telephone and called the fire department and in minutes we had these big hulking guys in all of their fireman gear chopping holes in our dining room wall to let the water out. Then they brought in huge bags of sawdust and covered the floor with it and vacuumed it all up. The rain stopped and the flooding threat was over. We profusely thanked them, thank you, thank you, thank you. We were so tired we probably sounded like fools. They all clamored and clanked their way out of the house, got in their big red noisy truck and drove away. We never received anything from the fire department, not a bill, not a statement, not a thing. What a country we live in, we're blessed. The remodel was supposed to take six months but it stretched into a year. I learned then, too late, that a contract should have a completion clause. Between working at the studio and fighting with the contractor we were ready for a break.

Beauty and the Beast was the first animated film in history to be nominated for an Oscar for best picture. Being a member of the Academy I was allowed to vote for the picture. I had my ballot but I had let the time slip by and had forgotten to mail it in. There was no time to lose so Vera and I took a lunch break, jumped on the freeway, and hurried over to Los Angeles. We drove into the underground parking of the building that housed Price Waterhouse, the keepers of the ballots. We hurried to the elevator, pushed the lobby button and rose up to step out into a lobby without a soul in sight. There was no one else in the building, not a soul, just us. We scampered over to building entrance to look out on the street level and saw yellow, police crime scene tape, stretched across the walk in front of the building. We were on the crime side of the crime scene tape! Very confused and worried, we didn't know what was going on. We were worried that we wouldn't get our ballot delivered on time or maybe get blown up.

Across the street from the building, we saw hundreds of people crowding the sidewalks. Suddenly we were startled by a loud voice behind us and we turned to see a security officer who blurted out that there was a bomb threat and the building had been evacuated. There we were alone, in this huge empty building with my ballot squeezed into my sweaty palm and no way to get up to Price Waterhouse to get my vote counted. The guard ushered us to the massive front door and told us to get across the street as quickly as possible. I guess we didn't look like part of a bomb threat and all of the people on the other side of the street welcomed us as if we were one of them. Vera and I looked at each other like "what now?" She suggested we ask the people in the crowd if anyone worked at Price Waterhouse; we asked dozens of people but none of them did. It was a very big building with many offices. We kept wandering among the crowd questioning people. We were very excited when we came to a group of ladies who all said they worked for Price Waterhouse. Of course when we told them that we worked for Walt Disney we were suddenly thought of as famous. When we told the ladies we needed someone to deliver our ballot, which was a vote for *Beauty and the Beast* to win an Oscar they were thrilled to help. Vera and I were greatly relieved. The crowd of people had started back into their building having been told that the bomb scare was called off, no bomb was found. We found our car in the underground parking and hurried off to Burbank to finish our afternoon's work.

A bigger and better wrap party was held to celebrate the successful

Vera and friends at Jeffrey's Oscar party

completion of *Beauty and the Beast*. The cast and crew gathered at the Universal Sheraton Hotel in Universal City for an evening of schmoozing, dining and dancing. After that the studio flew a group of us to Florida to celebrate with the Florida crew that had helped on the picture. We stayed at the Floridian Hotel which made us all feel pretty special. At the Disney Hollywood Studios, there at the Florida park, the street scene from the movie where Belle lived had been constructed as a movie set. That was where we had our very special wrap party. The street was populated with goats and horses with shops of the period and actors that played the townspeople. And of course at the end of the evening, to celebrate the movie, there was an enormous fireworks display which lit up that whole sky over the fake Disney World city of Hollywood.

On Oscar night Jeffrey Katzenberg held a party at a big restaurant in Hollywood for all of the film's artists. The television presentation of the Oscar ceremonies was presented on a huge screen big enough for all to see.

It was a fun night but we were all very disappointed when the Oscar for best picture wasn't captured by *Beauty and the Beast*.

Beauty and the Beast was released November 21, 1991. It didn't win for Best Picture but it won awards for Best Music and Best Original Score. The first year of release it was reported to have earned $145 million, domestic. Vera had successfully supervised the clean up department and we were both proud to have been a part of that movie.

My earlier decision to resign the post as supervisor of effects had future painful consequences. In 1992 a book was published with the title, *Disney's*

Art of Animation: From Mickey Mouse to Beauty and the Beast, by Bob Thomas. There is a section in the book which presents the whys and wherefores of special effects animation. My name isn't in it. Randy Fullmer, who took over as effects supervisor after I stepped down has his picture presented as well as a small blurb of his history. Vera also has her picture in the book with praise as supervisor of the clean up crew. I'm proud of these guys. However for me, I still have severe artist ego damage. But life must always be ever onward and upward, hopefully.

After working those long days, weeks, and months on *Beauty and the Beast,* Vera and I had plans to run away to Hawaii to play for a couple weeks. Three days before we were to leave for Hawaii a hurricane moved up from the south Pacific and decided to vacation in Hawaii. Hurricane Iniki was a direct hit on the Island of Kauai. I later saw a satellite photo that showed Iniki just a little bigger than the island of Kauai, the hurricane centered right on top of the island, bull's eye fashion. Vera and I came home from work that day and turned on the news to see television shots from a helicopter flying right along the beach leading to our Nihi Kai Village condo complex. Naturally we were alarmed and didn't know what to do about our trip. We didn't even know if we had a condo anymore. As we watched the TV footage I noticed that the film would cut just before the helicopter got to our condo. I said to Vera, "Hey, you know the news people, if it bleeds it reads, and they only want to show what's damaged and bleeding, sad and depressing. They don't want to show you boring okay stuff so they stop before they get to our condo because it's okay!" Vera thought that sounded right.

The morning after the hurricane I dialed Nancy Grantham's cell phone number in Koloa, Hawaii. Nancy owned Grantham Resorts, the management company that managed our condo. I dialed her cell phone as a long shot, never dreaming I could connect, but she answered the call. She and her husband Bruce had just walked out of the house to survey the hurricane damage. I couldn't believe that cell phone technology. I told her about our plans to come over to Maui and she liked the idea. Our friends on Kauai needed friends to talk to for they had no TV, no movies, and no restaurants; it was almost Stone Age. Vera and I changed our flight and took off for Maui. We stayed at The Whaler, a condo resort on Kaanapali Beach on Maui, and kept in touch with our folks on Kauai to see when it would be all clear for us to come over.

After about three days of playing in the sunshine of Maui while our friends on Kauai lived in the dark, without electricity, we got word that power was on there and we could get a flight to Kauai. Our condo was between the main power source on that side of the island and the new beautiful Grand Hyatt Kauai Resort on the beach just east of our condo complex. The hotel employed lots of people and the damage was mostly confined to the beautiful acres of porcelain tile on the roof and all of the vegetation and tropical fish ponds on the property. Tourism is the main source of income and jobs on the island so the hotel had enough clout to make sure they could get the electricity on so their workers could get back to earning a living by taking care of the tourists. Because our condo was on the power system that ran to the hotel, we had power when the hotel got theirs.

We were relieved to see that our condo had only suffered slight damage. The ridge cap of the Spanish tiled roof had blown off. The rain had poured in through the holes in the ceiling and stained our walls and soaked the furniture causing stains in all of the carpets. There were many Kama'aina, the Hawaiian word for "those that have lived here a long time," local people, who had their houses destroyed so I did feel a bit guilty about that. The little vacation rental houses on the road that ran along the beach by our condo complex were lifted off their foundations by the hurricane and moved about a hundred feet inland. The asphalt road had been lifted up and moved inland about forty feet. I heard that the waves crossing that beach had reached thirty feet high during hurricane Iniki. The asphalt lay in large chunks on the ground where the houses once stood. It looked like some sort of giant puzzle with what was the yellow center line skipping and zigzagging across the big pieces of the errant asphalt chunks. The big dirt scar where the road had been was piled with boulders as big as truck tires.

Our Nihi Kai condo complex swimming pool was half filled with huge rocks and debris along with all of the patio furniture which our resident

Nihi Kai Villas after hurricane Iniki

137

manager was smart enough to throw into the pool to keep it from blowing into the buildings, breaking windows and such.

One evening, during that first visit after the hurricane, we invited our resident manager over for drinks and while sitting on the lanai it started raining one of those tropical downpours. Suddenly we were literally sitting behind a waterfall as the rain water poured off the roof. In the living room we had placed at least a dozen big buckets to catch the water from the leaking ceiling and they were filling up fast. Fortunately the rain stopped as suddenly as it had begun, as those tropical downpours do, and the waterfall subsided. We didn't have another downpour like that until the condo complex had been restored to its original splendor.

I had saved all of my paperwork relating to the expenses and income for the rental of the condo so the Allstate Insurance Company was very cooperative. We had everything repainted and had new carpeting installed and bought new furniture. The condo association fixed the roof and took care of all exterior repairs so we were in business again. It only took about seven months to get it all put back together. We were a long time out of the condo business but the insurance people paid us for the tourist rent we lost for the seven months. It could have been a lot worse. Sadly, for many of the islanders it was.

All of the piles of tons and tons of debris from destroyed trees, buildings and houses, refrigerators, stoves and furniture, were all buried in very large holes on the back side of the island. The island is about thirty-three miles across so it had a lot of space for holes. Almost all of the houses were rebuilt with new roofs. Vacation homes were built along the new road leading to our condo where the old homes had been demolished by the hurricane. The island looked better than ever. The next time Vera and I flew over to Kauai, after everything was rebuilt, we were coming in for a landing and Vera said, "It's beautiful; all of the houses have new hats on!"

CHAPTER 16

Aladdin and the Ride on the Magic carpet

Vera began working with the directors, Ron Clements and John Musker again, this time on *Aladdin*. She was happy about that and happy that she would be credited as the Artistic Supervisor of the clean up department. I was content to sit in my room, at my desk, animating special effects, sheltered from most of the political breezes. Before we had finished *Beauty and the Beast*, the effects department was moved out of the parking lot, out of the pre-fab building, and into the real Flower Street building where I had my own corner room. The interior of the building was remodeled to make it look like a little village with a series of shops or little house offices.

Looking back it seems, for me, *Aladdin* was a rather uneventful picture to work on. It was fun, it was good, but since I didn't have the cheerleader, supervising chore, there was just work to do. I was out of the drama business. There were no jarring political experiences to impinge my memory banks or huge effects scenes. Don Paul was the effects supervisor in California and Barry Cook was effects supervisor in Florida, until Jeff Dutton took over. Those guys had the job of exciting the artists to the frenzy required for getting the special effects completed.

At the beginning of a picture the pressure was usually minimal but I was getting tired of the long drive to the studio. The Ventura Freeway seemed to be more crowded every day. I think Vera loved our house on the hill more than she disliked the drive but for me it was the other way around. We would leave for work at about six forty five in the morning and get to the studio in time to have breakfast at WDI, the Walt Disney Imagineering commissary, on Flower Street, across from our studio. We would usually get there by seven thirty, if there were no collisions on the freeway.

Remodeling our Woodland Hills house turned it into a great party house. Vera enjoyed throwing parties and we always had a big one on the Forth of July. Our backyard looked down on Pierce College and each July Forth there would be sky divers jumping out of aircraft above our swimming pool.

Our backyard party pool

After the sun went down there would be a fireworks show that illuminated our back yard as the bursts exploded high above the pool. I had a bunch of CDs with John Philip Sousa marching music, including my favorite, the Monty Python theme song *Liberty Bell*. I blasted the marching music out over the pool all day long to instill the proper Independence Day spirit.

I remember having Joe Ranft and his wife Sue out to the house for parties. They were great fun. Joe Raft was a Disney artist and storyteller at Walt Disney Feature Animation and contributed to many of the hits including *The Lion King*. He left Disney to work at Pixar where he contributed greatly to the stories of the Pixar hits. The animation world was shocked and grieved on August 16, 2005, when the news was released that we had lost Joe in a car accident. He was Co-Director with John Lasseter on *Cars* and the movie was dedicated to him. An amazing talent and good, decent person gone, but his work lives on.

In the early 1970's, before all of the Pixar hits and before the computer boom, I attended a seminar at USC where all of the latest computer animation projects were presented. The star of the show was a film which had an animated fly-thru of a greatly simplified town, just geometric shapes with holes for doors and windows. I heard that the film effort, which was about three minutes long, cost ten million dollars to make. I was working at the time for Film Designers, our little film company, owned by Educational Materials Company out of Minneapolis, Minnesota. Over in Beverly Hills there was a company financed by the Smothers Brothers. They were attempting to develop what they called "Disney quality character animation." The company invited me and my partners over to Beverly Hills to view their efforts hoping that if we did a film we might be able to use their program, whatever that was. Their building was beautiful with a walnut paneled screening room and a powered drop-down screen. The Smothers Brothers used the Tiffany style for their décor on their TV show so that style was prevalent throughout the offices for lamps and glass panels. We all gathered in the screening room and as the film began we watched a bird-like creature hobble across the screen from one side to the other. I was not impressed nor were my partners. We were then invited upstairs to visit the tiny little room where there was a camera and the equipment used to get the bird on the screen. The gentleman showing us the computer equipment was obviously impressed with what they were doing but one of my guys, the more business directed of us, said, "Gee, I'm totally under whelmed," emphasizing "under." That company was eventually sold and melded into the many companies that were beginning to explore the computer's usefulness for film work at the time. It was all a beginning to the future which led to the amazing work of John Lasseter and helped to kick off all of the computer graphics, CG, film work that is being done today.

Aladdin had some of the first character animation work done with computers. Tina Price developed the process and animated the flying carpet using the computer. All of that carpet detail would have been a 2d artist's nightmare and wouldn't have looked as precise or attractive. Tina is a very talented artist and computer animation pioneer; She is the founder of The Creative Talent Network (CTN), which showcases animation talent in extravagant affairs. In November 2009, Tina produced histories first ever CTN Animation Expo. It was staged in Burbank California and was a super success which brought hundreds of artists from around the world together for three days to show portfolios, share knowledge, talent, and experience, as well as to renew friendships. Throughout it all there was a communal passion for animation. The success of that event, along with a city proclamation for "Animation Week", has promised us that the CTN Animation Expo will be an annual event into the future. And we have Tina Price and her endless energy and talent to thank for that as well as her love of the art of animation and animation artists.

Aladdin was released November 25, 1992 and the box office for domestic theaters was $217 million and it earned about the same amount in the rest of the world. That was a total gross of almost a half billion dollars, a very successful big hit movie. Eric Goldberg animated the outrageous Genie with a whacky Robin Williams acting the voice over. The Los Angeles *Aladdin* wrap party should have been notable for me but there have been so many big parties that some of them are just all floating together in the party river of my mind. I do remember that Vera and I were invited to Florida to celebrate the finish of *Aladdin* with the Florida crew there. We partied in Morocco at the World Showcase. It was a cold night for Florida but inside the restaurant in Morocco the food was delicious and it was warm enough for scantily dressed belly dancers to display their wares. It was very special evening which we all enjoyed but I still wonder why I can't remember the wrap party we had in Los Angeles.

CHAPTER 17

My Pride With the Lions

Vera agreed to give up our nice Woodland Hills house on the hill and move to Glendale; I think she was tired of hearing me complain about the long drive to Burbank. The studio was doing well so it looked like we would be working in Burbank for awhile. In Vera's spare time she set out with a prominent Glendale real estate agent, Gerri Cragnotti, to find a house for us in Glendale. When Vera found something she liked and thought I would like, she would set up an appointment for us to go tour the house together, so we ended up buying a house we both liked. It was on the northwest corner of Cumberland Road and Ard Eevin Avenue, ten minutes from the studio. The house had been built in 1936 by superior craftsman unlike those un-craftsmen-like guys that remodeled our Woodland Hills house. It had thick lathe and plaster walls, was very sound proof, fairly large and closer to work. Before moving to Glendale we hired a real estate agent friend to find someone who would rent our Woodland Hills house. We wanted to keep it as an investment. He found a really sweet French couple who paid us a security deposit and the first month's rent.

Living in Glendale allowed us to love our much-shorter drive to work. We raved about it so much that Don Hahn and his wife Denise decided to move to Glendale from Santa Clarita, not long after we moved in. They moved into a really nice big spectacular house on the opposite corner, one block west of us and then remodeled it to be an even bigger, more spectacular house, as only Don could do.

Vera and I moved into our Cumberland house around April of 1993 and were very comfortable there until 4:31 in the morning of January 17, 1994. That's when the house started roaring and shaking, rattling and breaking. The

Northridge Earthquake decided to visit us with a 6.7 on the MMS scale. That means it's frightening. The pantry unloaded its shelves, and the Spanish tile on the living room roof, an area of about one-hundred fifty square feet, decided to slip off the house and onto the ground. Our fireplace had a very large, very heavy, brick chimney cap which decided to fall over on to the living room roof and punch a large hole in our nice vaulted ceiling. We had a security system and because the shaking was so literally deafening I didn't know the alarm was going until the house stopped ripping, roaring and shaking. Only then could I hear that the alarm was piercingly loud.

The earthquake caused Vera to become physically sick enough that we drove over to Saint Joseph's hospital in Burbank to see a doctor in the emergency room. There were a dozen or so people in the waiting room with various injuries, mostly all minor cuts and scrapes. I do remember my disgust when somebody had bled all over the floor and the people in the room, kind of in a fearful daze, kept tracking through the puddle. They just stared at me like zombies when I would try to steer them around the blood. I purchased a 7-Up for Vera for we thought she might be suffering from low blood sugar, she had experienced that before. The 7-Up seemed to help a bit. I think that most of those people in the waiting room were just afraid to be at home, it was a very scary morning. Vera felt better after drinking the 7-Up, and we thought she would feel even better if we just got away from the scared people waiting to see a doctor. We went back home to inspect the remodeling that the earthquake had decided our house needed and were fairly stunned by the result. Thankfully it was mostly cosmetic and could have been much worse.

Our house in Northridge, near the center of the quake, where Vera's folks lived and the apartment in Encino where Vera's sister lived with her three kids, were all damaged slightly but enough to make it unsafe until some repairs were made. I think everyone was afraid to be alone so Vera and I had six people, Vera's mom, dad, sister and the three kids, move in with us. I set about hiring people to fix things.

To add more problems to our situation, that sweet French couple who had rented our Woodland Hills house failed to pay the rent after the first month. So for the six months before the earthquake Vera and I had been dealing with the sheriff's office, the bankruptcy courts and the total frustration of a government system that allows shiftless tenants to steal a house from responsible landlords. Our renters were advised by a law group who help people stay in a rental house without paying rent. Yikes!

I went out to Woodland Hills to check on our house there, those scumbags who had presented themselves as a sweet French couple had moved out. The only damage was a broken window. I still wonder why those deceitful people left the house so clean, without a speck of trash or dirt. They basically stole eight thousand dollars from Vera and I plus the time we had to spend in court. They didn't show up at the hearing, disappeared from Los Angeles, and never honored the court order to pay us.

Fortunately, we weren't into overtime at the studio so the domestic problems and earthquake damage were easier to deal with. Vera and I, as supervisor of clean up and effects animator respectively, were both working on *The Lion King*. It was hard work pleasing the directors but no harder than hiring people to fix our houses. We even lost our cat Taco during this period, the one that saved us from confronting a burglar. Vera's mom had volunteered to take care of Taco after we came back from Europe and Taco learned how to unlatch the back screen door to go out in the yard and lay in the sun. One day the gardeners came ripping into the yard with the lawn mower and Taco went over the wall and that was that. Vera and I had a bit of guilt from that too because we didn't bring Taco home with us when moved to our house on the hill. He was a great mysterious cat with some strange connection to the universe and burglars, but we never saw him again.

The earthquake damage was being repaired but Vera's mom had started feeling sickly when she was living with us. I got the houses fixed up and everyone went back home but Vera's mom required surgery for a large tumor that she had acquired. After her surgery she was okay but the docs suggested chemo and that was that. We lost her March, 1994. That call came early in the morning. Vera and I had rushed to the hospital but we were too late: the Josie we knew left us minutes after we got there. Vera was close to her mom and the loss was devastating for her. She had discussed chemo with her mom and she had decided it was the thing for her Mom to do so she felt an enormous burden of responsibility for the outcome. Ahead of her was a long period of sadness and grief. I wasn't as much help as Vera needed for I just wanted to get on with it, Josie wasn't coming back, but Vera just wasn't herself. She was grief stricken. Vera was a long time getting her happy spirit back and things were never quite the same after that.

Long before Vera and I moved to Glendale, we were invited to the first pitch of *The Lion King* story to the crew and far from being impressed, we were both disappointed. We discussed the story on the way home and both felt the story needed a lot of work. But the history of that movie illustrates that making an animated feature is usually more of a process than a live action film. Instead of starting with a script it starts with an idea for a story, no script. And because the art is so important in the telling of the story, the picture develops as a series of story board sketches. After thousands and thousands of sketches are pinned up, the story ideas pitched, thousands of sketches taken down, pinned up, taken down and thrown away a movie begins to take form.

Once we were into actually animating the movie, Don Hahn, the producer of *The Lion King*, brought a very attractive little actress into my room so I could show her some effects animation drawings and how it all worked. I had animated the ghost Mufasa where he rises up in the sky so I would flip the drawings for her. She was a popular Japanese movie star and exhibited that confident movie star quality. She had an interpreter with her who was an American. He had lived in Japan for years and traveled with her for this trip. I quickly learned that when the interpreter would, in Japanese, tell her what I had said it was her clue to become an exuberant, excited movie star acting totally impressed with what we were showing her. She became the show; *The Lion King* was her stage and I was her prop. The process was fun to watch. I have a video of the Japanese television show where they used the film footage we shot that day of me showing the actress drawings and her emoting. It was a piece promoting Disney and *The Lion King*. In the video I am amusingly speaking Japanese for they had dubbed in a Japanese actor's voice over mine.

The Lion King was directed by Rob Minkoff and Roger Allers. It was an enormous success when it was released on June 24, 1994. It won two Oscars, Best Music, Original Score and Best Music, Original Song, *Can You Feel the LoveTonight,* by Elton John and Tim Rice. After *The Lion King* was finished we had a huge wrap party in Pasadena at a vacant mansion. It was an elaborate affair and I remember it well. Jeffrey Katzenberg and his wife Marilyn, along with Roy Disney and his wife Patty, were stationed on the patio where they were greeting everyone after we had wandered through the mansion to get to the backyard patio and a very large backyard. There was an abundance of food and many dancers and singers, all in African style outfits, entertaining in the spacious yard. The only unusual part of the evening was provided by a company that provided outdoor relief stations. For reasons never revealed to me, or maybe I just didn't know where the bathrooms were and they needed extra ones, there was a group of portable potties at an obscure location on the property. I remember when I first had to use one I had wandered alone and found the portable out houses, with no one waiting. When I finished and opened the door to exit, there was a group of people who had lined up waiting for a vacant potty. It startled me, they were all looking anxiously at me, so as I paused with the door open I said, "Hey, I thought this was the flight to Chicago." Well, everyone laughed so the pre-potty tension was tempered and I don't think I had to find that station again during the rest of the evening. It was an evening to remember but Vera and I had a few more ahead of us.

After that party Vera and I were invited to go to New York for the *The Lion King* opening in the Radio City Music Hall at Rockefeller Center. We sat in the first row center of the balcony with a few other Disney folks along on that trip and watched a stage presentation followed by a screening of our movie. We had a wrap party after the screening in what was the ice rink, in the winter, across the street from the Center. We stayed at the Hotel Regency on Park Avenue but while in New York Vera was still grieving about losing her mother and kept her feelings pretty much suppressed. When all the festivities had ceased Vera and I checked out of the hotel wearing our Lion King hats. As we approached the cab which would scurry us to JFK the cab driver noticed our hats and began raving about them so Vera took hers off and gave it to a very gracious cabby. Our schedule called for us to be in Florida for *The Lion King* wrap party there, so off we went, JFK to Orlando Florida. The date was June 17, 1994. I know because when we got to our hotel at Disney World I turned on the TV to catch the news. OJ Simpson was taking a drive in Al Cowlings white Bronco on a Los Angeles freeway.

The Florida wrap party for *The Lion King* was in an enormous building somewhere around the Yacht Club Hotel. That part of Disneyworld seems to be deceptive for there are large buildings that aren't visible until you're in one. The entrance to the building was decorated with jungle foliage and a big tree with a very large lion model, which looked real, lying in the tree over the doors. The party was different from most for there were games with Velcro suits. One would put on the Velcro suit then throw one's self against a Velcro wall to see how high one could stick. There were many games of that nature and of course lots of food and beverages. Even Jeffrey Katzenberg was there participating. After that party our feelings of special-ness had to be put on the back burner until we finished another successful movie. This time we had a Native American waiting for us with the name of *Pocahontas*.

The Lion King was released in June of 1994, and after the enormous success of over a half billion dollars the artists were informed that Peter and Jeffrey would be handing out bonuses in Peter's office. Of course there was some sort of pecking order so it was the animators and supervisors who would be directly rewarded by Peter and Jeffrey with a warm hand shake and a "thank you, what a wonderful job you did on the picture." It was very special for me. Everyone else, the assistants and follow up artists would receive their bonuses in their mailbox. Even at that it took most of the day for Peter and Jeffrey to get through all the animators and supervisors with a personal thank you and a check. We had to mill about in an orderly fashion in the lobby of the building until our name was called. Most people would come out of Peter's office with a pleased smile on their face and move out of building without revealing their bonus amount.

Later that day I happened to see Vera pulling her Plymouth Voyager into the parking lot across from the Flower Street studio. As supervisor of the clean up department she was in charge of the artists whose job was to redraw all of the drawings in the film so it looked like one person did them. She was returning from her visit with Peter and Jeffrey. I hurried across the street to greet her, anxious to compare notes on our bonuses. She jumped out of her van with a look on her face as if she had won a lottery. In her hand was a large white envelope which she was waving wildly. I said, "How did you do?" And peering up at me with a gleeful look on her face and without speaking a word she pulled a check from the envelope to show me. Printed on the check was an amount which was enough to buy a new Jaguar XK8. Finally the studio was recognizing the importance of Vera as a great clean up artist, and my bonus? I don't remember how much it was; I surely would have remembered if it had been a larger amount.

CHAPTER 18
Native Americans
and Notre Dame

The year 1994 wasn't working for Vera and I. Vera was getting more distraught and I was bewildered by it all. Years ago there was a radio personality who I heard say, "Putting a failed relationship back together between a man and a woman is like trying to rebuild a cobweb." Vera was still grieving for her mom and I was just trying to get on with things. One day I came home from work and Vera had placed all of what she had referred to as my "crazy books", books of Buddhism, philosophy and psychology, on the kitchen table. I had told her that those crazy books helped me get my life together and now it appeared that she planned on finding her peace in those books.

Early on when I heard the first pitch the story guys had constructed for our film, *Pocahontas*, I was reminded of the stories I had read over the years. No one ever asked me to be a story man but I had to put my two cents in. I looked up the story in the set of encyclopedias that I had given Vera as a gift and discovered that it was a very interesting story, more interesting than the story I remembered. How would a teenage Native American girl rise to such prominence? I sat down and wrote a short treatment for the story based on my research with Vera's encyclopedias and sent a copy to Jim Pentecost, the film's producer. I was told later that they used some of my ideas, but of course I would like to think they used my whole idea. I'm sure there are a lot of story guys including Tom Sito, who was head of story on that picture, who would see it differently. I was an effects animator, not a story man.

The only major effect I remember animating on the picture was the waterfall at which *Pocahontas* appears when John Smith finds her. Mostly there was a lot of water to do, some leaves blowing and shadows here and there.

The studio had mentioned to both Vera and I that they would like for us to go to Paris to work on *The Hunchback of Notre Dame.* I don't remember Vera and me even discussing it. The stresses were beginning to cause us to lose whatever it was we had. We heard nothing more about going to Paris until one day we were invited to talk to the lady in charge of those things and she informed us that she had our airline tickets for France. I was not happy about the studio assuming we would be thrilled to go live in France without even a meeting to discuss it, some one had forgotten to call us. We hadn't even really settled into our Glendale house. We had visited Paris a few times and it was a fun place but we had made no plans to move there. I stated as such to the lady in charge and that was the end of that.

Christmas that year was not a merry one for me or Vera. In January 1995, Peter Schneider had invited us to the Golden Globe Awards ceremony because *The Lion King* had been nominated for several categories, including Best Picture. I refused to go. Vera and I had been testy with each other and because of that I didn't think it would be a fun evening, especially at a black tie, formal affair, like the Golden Globe Awards ceremony. Vera was determined to go so she invited Marshall Toomey, a friend and fellow artist, much bigger, black, and more handsome than me, to accompany her. In fact, Vera and I are the godparents of Marshall's son, TC.

Some humor resulted from that evening's paring of Vera and Marshall, at least for me. The next day I ran into Peter and he said "Dorse, you didn't look like yourself last night." I said to Peter, without explanation, "Peter, that was a special effects trick." He chuckled in passing for we were on our way somewhere without time for explanations. *The Lion King* won the Golden Globe award that night for Best Motion Picture, Best Original Score and what seemed like an ironic point to be made for me that evening, Best Song, *Can You Feel the Love Tonight.*

A few months later Vera and I failed to iron out our differences, we couldn't seem to get over the bump and decided to split up. A few weeks later at a studio party, as Peter was leaving, he signaled a "call me" hand sign as he walked out the door. I called him later and he invited me to have breakfast at Chez Nous Restaurant in Toluca Lake to express his regrets. He had heard that Vera and I were breaking up, interesting term, breaking up. Just like a ship at sea being pounded to pieces by the waves.

There was a New York outdoor screening in Central Park of *Pocahontas*, to kick off the release of the film. That was a public affair which I didn't attend. The picture was released on June 23, 1995. Its box office just couldn't top *The Lion King* which was now the champion to beat. The Los Angeles wrap party was a splendid affair held at The Union Station, the big railroad station in downtown, the studio had taken over the whole beautiful interior for the party. The highlight of the party for me was that I met John Lasseter for the first time.

In April, Vera went to France to work on Hunchback and I was shuffling around looking for a ladder that I could use to climb out of the hole I was in; time to reinvent myself, again. I was working on *The Hunchback of Notre Dame* and she was going to France to help the crew at the studio there. I called the movers and moved out of the house and into The Kenwood Mews Apartments in Burbank. The apartments were nice but I wasn't emotionally prepared to be back in an apartment.

The not very amusing for me, Kenwood Mews Apartments

Vera had signed a paper saying I could take anything from the house that I needed. I took a sofa, TV and video tapes. I went to Bed Bath and Broke, as I called it, and bought a few cooking utensils. My friend Thad said the apartment complex I had moved into was for show biz people on the way up or on the way out. I was on the way down.

After a couple of days I sort of got settled in my new, tiny, one-bedroom apartment and prepared to calculate my future. One evening there was a knock on the door. Who knew? I went to the door and it was fellow friend and effects animator Dan Lund, with a house warming gift, a six foot tall ficus tree in a big plastic pot, a living reminder that things could be worse. I still have that tree in my living room and I've "bonsai'd" it so it's still 6 feet tall in the same size pot, but now it's a nice, ceramic porcelain, pot.

The Von's market was a short walk from my apartment so one evening I decided to walk to the market to get something for dinner and some coffee. I thought I would make pasta for dinner that evening. It's easy, quick and filling and the market sauces are all pretty good. So I said goodbye to my ficus and off to the market I went trying to feel spirited and upbeat instead of lonely and beat up. The market wasn't crowded at all so I grabbed what I needed and then stopped by the coffee isle. I really wasn't in the mood to talk to anyone, I just wanted to get my stuff and get back to my apartment. As I approached the coffee aisle there was a nice looking lady standing in front of the coffee. In order to reach my Folgers I had to say "Excuse me." The lady replied as she stepped aside, "Am I in your way?" I said "No." She quickly said "Would you like for me to be?" Yikes, I was so not tuned in to a pick up frame of mind that I gave her a quick "no," grabbed my coffee, turned and raced for the check out counter and never looked back. I was perversely amused by the fact that the universe had offered up a person to me for company at the very time in my life when I felt so un-wanting of it. I walked back to my apartment scratching my head in wonder, looking forward to a nice dish of pasta with extra sauce. I got back to my apartment, put the stuff away and started cooking the pasta. I began to feel like I was going to survive. Food to eat, coffee in the morning before heading off to a good, fun job, and a little gym downstairs where I was going to start working out. When the pasta was done cooking I realized that didn't have a strainer so I put a lid on the pasta pot and began to drain the pasta water into the garbage disposal. Opps, the pasta slipped out from under the lid of the pot and disappeared down the black hole of the garbage disposal. Umm, that was my pasta, gone. It was getting late, pasta needs time to cook and I needed rest. It was time to get in bed and pull the covers over my head like the curtain coming down on a really bad play.

CHAPTER 19

When the Saints Go Marching In

There were some fun effects to do in *The Hunchback of Notre Dame*. I began on the sequence of the Festival of Fun "topsy turvy" day, when the crowds made fun of Quasimodo. My head was a little less muddled now, after selling the properties, so my work was more fun. We animated the tomatoes and garbage the crowd of people shamelessly threw at the sympathetic Quasimodo. There were lots of fires and torches to do and many scenes required tone mattes and shadows. But my favorite scene, a sequence of scenes to animate, was when Quasimodo dumped the hot molten copper out of the towers of Notre Dame to drive away the guards below. It was a complicated scene which required a lot of very large drawings and some serious invention to make it work. I always liked doing effects for not only was there drawing to be done, but in a complex scene a great deal of invention was necessary to craft ways for the camera man to manipulate those drawings under the camera for maximum effect.

While I was working on the movie I was worrying about a tooth problem; I had a hole in a tooth that the dentist said happens mostly to children. The tooth starts dissolving, not a cavity, but rather just a hole that keeps getting bigger. The dentist had been treating it with a chemical that was supposed to stop it but the hole was getting bigger. One day while having a sandwich at a local restaurant, Talley Rand in Burbank, my tooth gave way and broke off. It was a lower front tooth, so I looked like a Milton Berle clown with a blacked out tooth; odd how lousy things happen when you need good things happening. So now not only did I feel like a loser, I looked like one. But only when I opened my mouth, so I tried to keep it shut. After a few trips to the dentist, some grinding, some caps and a single tooth bridge, I looked better

153

than ever for my lower teeth were all new, straight and shiny. The dentist said it would be good for ten years, that was about fourteen years ago.

During all of this hoopla my doctor, Doctor Kuraishi, recommended a counselor to help me get my head back on straight. After two visits with the counselor, me whining while he sat there collecting his money for listening to me whine, I decided that it wasn't a counselor I needed but a house to live in. I needed to look forward to the future and the counselor had me looking backward to the past; well it wasn't his fault for it was me dwelling in my past, whining. Remembering what the Greek philosopher Epectitus said, and thanks to my crazy books, I realized I needed a different view of life. So I changed my view of the landscape. I needed a nice house, in a nice neighborhood, filled with relatively normal people with relatively normal lives. That day I left the counselor's office and drove through some lovely neighborhoods of Glendale and Burbank looking for a house to buy. I never went back to the counselor and he never called me to ask if I had committed suicide or committed anything. How could he not be curious?

I called Gerri Cragnotti, my real estate agent and she was eager to help me start looking for a house. I drove alone through the streets of neighborhoods I found appealing, looking for signs which read For Sale. When I found a house I liked I would call Gerri, she would meet me there later and show me the interior and grounds. It was good therapy for me to drive by a zillion houses that I would like to own. We finally found a house I liked in the hills of Glendale, where I still live. Nice view of a distant downtown Los Angeles which I could see from the comfort of my breakfast room. I still have breakfast looking at the view and feel truly blessed that I don't have to live in a card board box on the streets of that big city, down there, like so many homeless people do. I moved in on October 22, 1995 and my divorce was final two days later. Being one who is not attracted to funny colors, frilly curtains and flowery wall paper, or hanging Italian lamps that looked like broken bottles, I started minor cosmetic remodeling, not only of the house, but the nooks and crannies of my own mind as well.

Back at the studio, the room I used when working on The *Hunchback of Notre Dame* was an interior room with no windows. Without a window I was always concerned that the world could disappear when I wasn't looking. If the world goes I want to be watching for it will no doubt be spectacular. I had noticed a room over on the other side of the building, two hallways away, that seemed to be unoccupied. It had a nice big window which looked out on Riverside Drive. The main lot was across the street with Mickey Mouse painted high up on the water tower where he could peer down on his domain and even look in the window of that seemingly unoccupied room. I wanted that room with a window. After some nosing around I found out that Dan

Hansen, a layout guy, was working in a room upstairs and the room with the window was his downstairs room if ever he had stuff to do downstairs, which was basically never. That seemed silly to me that he would have a room downstairs that had windows, he was never downstairs to look out a window. I knew if I went through the proper channels to acquire the room with the window it would no doubt become an issue of some sort. Some middle managers, like politicians, complicate things, for complication lends them maximum importance with minimal positive contribution. I talked to Dan and made my case. He could have my room on the ground floor without windows and I would move into the room with a big window and a view to the outside world. He went for the idea so I moved into that room with the big window and a view. No one ever complained about my migration. I think my fellow workers thought my upgraded room with the big window lent an air of importance to me which I never denied.

After *The Hunchback of Notre Dame* was in the can, the party planners planned a big wrap party to be held at the Shrine Auditorium in Los Angeles. Kirk Wise and Gary Trousdale had directed a wonderful fun version of that story and we all deserved a big party. We screened the movie there at the Shrine; it's a big place. Then afterward we partied in a really big room with tons of food, music, and hilarity. That evening was especially nice for we didn't have to drive from the screening to the party as we had done at other wrap party evenings; it was all in one building. We were so spoiled. Even though the movie didn't do as well at the box office as *The Lion King,* it was still a success. But none of our films completed after *The Lion King* matched the triumph of that block buster of a movie.

In June of 1996 *The Hunchback of Notre Dame* was going to premier in the New Orleans's Super Dome. Several thousand kids had been given tickets for the event. Six giant screens were suspended from the ceiling of the Super Dome so every seat in the big structure of the building would have a clear view of a very large screen. A group of the key artists from the studio were invited to attend. We were flown to New Orleans on two charter jets. We were honored with rooms in the New Orleans Holiday Inn which is just a short walk to the Super Dome. It was fun to be bussed to the backside of the Los Angeles International Airport, get off the bus and get on the plane, no waiting, no security.

Holly was loving it

The party planners had kindly thought of everything for the aircraft was supplied with a buffet of food and drinks so no one would go hungry. When we landed in New Orleans, again without the need for security checks, we departed the aircraft and boarded buses for the trip to the hotel.

This New Orleans trip was a most unusual experience for me because I decided to invite my granddaughter, Holly, along. I was now a single person without a companion and I was invited to take a guest on this trip so I chose her. She wasn't then, and isn't now, a shy person and was thrilled by the idea. She was eleven years old and I'm still not sure what the forces were that caused me to invite her along. I'm not a superstitions sort and still wonder about it. What was I going to do with an eleven-year-old girl who up to that point I had considered to be very bright but, well, bratty? I began to like my granddaughter before the plane left the ground and we had a great flight to New Orleans. We were given a nice room on the sixth floor of the Holiday Inn Hotel and in the room was a gift bag waiting for us with a camera and other goodies. Holly had her list of things to wear for each day and she was always ready to get out of bed, check her list of outfits that her mom had made for her, and prepare for a fun day.

We took a trip out into the swamps to see the alligators. We were awed to see big alligators jump up, totally out of the water, to rip whole chicken parts off the tour guide's stick dangling out over that dark swamp water. For safety the boat had large plastic panels attached to the railings to make sure that the alligators didn't become passengers. I wonder how many people were eaten before they got the idea for the panels. We drove by the pumping stations that kept New Orleans dry and caused me to think that building a city below sea level is pleading with the gods to call your bluff and do you in by flooding you out. We walked along the edge of the Mississippi River on a warm balmy New Orleans evening. We swam in the pool on top of the Holiday Inn Hotel. One evening Holly and I decided to have dinner in the hotel restaurant downstairs. We dined with Patti and Chris Conklin and across the room were Vera with her husband Jim and her new baby Michael. Holly was so endearing that evening for she leaned over to me and quietly asked if she could go say hi to Vera. Vera was always very attentive and playful with Holly when Vera and I were married. That night Holly's behavior showed us that she could be more grownup than her elders.

The morning of the day we were going to see our movie in the Super Dome there was a Disney parade with Disney characters, dancers, and marching musicians. We sat in bleachers and watched Kirk and Gary roll by on a wagon float.

Holly ready for the parade

We then boarded buses and were driven to the Super Dome with crowds of people on the sidewalks cheering us on. It seemed as if the whole city of New Orleans was out to celebrate with us. The crowd in the Super Dome was gigantic with thousands of people attending and all excited to see a Disney animated film. Holly and I wiggled our way through the pressing multitude and found our assigned seats at eye level with one of the six giant screens suspended out in the middle of the stadium in front of us. Our film was preceded by a stage show and after the show the film was screened for the crowd. When the film ended, and everyone finished their applause and cheering, we went up into the very large party areas of the building where there was tons of food and drink and fun games. I introduced Holly to Alan Menken as he was coming down the stairs. At the time he was the winner of more Oscars than any other living composer, all for Disney films. Holly was properly impressed. There were only two instances when I became a bit worried about my ability to handle an eleven-year-old girl in distress. The first time was that evening at the party when some adults got a little rowdy and Holly began to feel a bit insecure. I was relieved and delighted when we were able to smooth over the moment and did not allow it to interfere with our celebration.

The next morning Holly and I decided to have breakfast in the hotel restaurant downstairs. We chose an empty table and began chatting about the movie. We were pleasantly pleased when the art director of our film, Dave Goetz, walked up to the table and asked if he could join us. After a few getting to know you quips Dave ask Holly what she thought of *The Hunchback of Notre Dame* as a movie. Dave was fairly confounded when words too wise for an eleven-year-old spilled out of Holly's mouth. She said, "I thought it was a good movie but the art of the buildings didn't work well with the character's style." She was referring to the computer construction of the church and surrounding buildings which she felt was an art style which conflicted with the design of the cartoon characters. I was proud and pleasingly embarrassed by Holly's boldness. Holly further explained what she meant and we had a fun breakfast with Dave. I think he respected her opinion.

The second time I had to smooth Holly's feathers was when there was to be an adult-only dinner party to be held in what I understood was at one time the governor's mansion. Paul Prudhomme, the famous chef, was doing the cooking. I think it was Cajun food but I've read that most all of the cooking in New Orleans is Creole. The stories I've read about the difference between Cajun and Creole leaves me scratching my head; It has something to do with the French first settling New Orleans and then the Spaniards became prominent and they all partied with the many black people who were part of the mix from the beginning. And now the best part is that it's just a colorful city with a blend of colorful people making great music and food. The Disney crew had set up one of the big rooms in the hotel with a few adults to supervise a children's party with games and toys with which the children could amuse themselves. I'm always amazed at how many really very big rooms a hotel can have in a building. Grandpa was amazed but Holly wasn't. Not by the size of the room or the kids at the party that were younger than her.

Ready for the kid's party

She didn't think it was going to be much fun, even in a really big room, in a really big hotel. We were lucky that Eric Daniels was there with his wife Marge and their daughter. Eric is a supremely talented artist and computer whiz who has worked at Disney for years and Marge is a fine painter as well as a character clean up artist at the studio. Eric also plays a mean ragtime piano. Their daughter was about Holly's age so Holly relaxed when she met them and the two girls hit it off. And off I went to a buffet style dinner of delicious Cajun food. Or was it Creole?

It was later that evening that all of us who had attended the dinner walked down to the river and boarded a paddle wheeler, the Cajun Queen. We floated off down the river while strains of New Orleans jazz drifted through the air along with the smoke from the cigars that Marshall Toomey was sharing with us. He had brought along his portable cigar humidor just for the occasion, a man of constant class. Even some of the ladies participated in the smoke fest.

I did miss another party one evening when everyone went down to Bourbon Street and partied into the early hours. I later heard that Peter was very generous with drinks all around and after talking to people about how much fun it was I was sorry I didn't get to participate in the festivities. But I was being Grandpa. Holly and I had a wonderful dinner at a nice restaurant that evening, maybe it was the Allegro Bistro, not sure now. It was fun watching my eleven-year-old grand daughter enjoy my company while dining on her Creole-or-was-it-Cajun food. She was being an adorable fancy grownup girl.

The last evening in New Orleans, Holly and I had our dinner in the revolving restaurant on the top of the hotel. It was special. Every revolution of the restaurant sent us passed the dessert station displaying a plethora of pies, cakes and artistic assorted chocolate enticements. And of course we had to react each time we past those sweet delights, and we did sample our share. As the sun was setting lower with each revolution, the city below became more orange and a little darker with a few more lights sparkling here and there. In the distance, Ole Man River, the big Mississippi, just kept rollin' along. Soon it was time to go. The next day we were bused to the airport to board the jets which would fly us back to L.A. The seats of the aircraft were first come first serve so as we boarded, Holly, walking in front of me as the spirited child she was, dove into two seats in the first class section. So we flew back in comfort reminiscing about our spectacular trip. When we arrived home it was planned for her to spend the night with me and her folks would pick her up the next day. The next day when Holly's parents arrived, my daughter Lisa and son-in-law Rick, I noticed a nuanced deterioration of my closeness to Holly. Her parents were the boss now. That moment didn't change our future relationship for we are still as close as a grandpa and granddaughter should be and she is on her way to becoming a successful artist.

CHAPTER 20

Hercules Takes Me to a New York Party

After *The Hunchback of Notre Dame,* we started work on our next film, *Hercules.* Another John Musker, Ron Clements, directed film with a style of its own. Mauro Maressa was the effects supervisor and James Mansfield and I were supervising effects animators. Gerald Scarfe, a world-renowned cartoonist, was the production designer. I hadn't done my homework so I really didn't know Mr. Scarfe. I was familiar with some of his work but wasn't aware of his success in the art world. One day as I sat working at my desk a man appeared at my door. As I've said before, I always worked with my door open unless I had a visitor in my room that needed to be talked to, or talked with, or maybe even someone who needed a shoulder to cry on, or maybe all three at the same time. Well, the man at the door who I thought was older than I just said hi, without an introduction. He and I had a little chat of very little substance and he never did say why he was there or who he was and I was kinda busy so I didn't ask. Turned out I missed my chance to have a serious talk with Gerald Scarfe. After I found out who the man was at my door I felt a bit foolish. I regret now that I never tracked him down to say hi and never had that opportunity again.

In April of 1996 my daughter felt that it wasn't good for me to live alone so she suggested that since her neighbor had two sister cats that had litters on the same day I could have two cats for the price of free. You know, one cat would need the company of another cat and the two cats would be my company. *Hercules* was demanding long work days so I would leave home at seven thirty in the morning and get home at ten or eleven o'clock in the

161

evening. The kittens, Maryann and Ginger, were about six week's old and loved living in my house. They spent a lot more time there that I did. It was as if they owned the place. The cats' coloring reminded a writer friend, Jeff Van Tuyl, of the girls on the TV show Gilligan's Island. On that show the character Ginger wore a beige spaghetti strap dress and Mary Ann was in a white blouse and black shorts. So the names stuck. Jeff gets the credit; I guess that's a writing credit.

That October, as we celebrated Halloween at the studio, a lady appeared at my door with a toddler in a stroller. As I looked up I was surprised to see that it was Vera with her baby Michael. She was wearing a white top with dalmatian-like black spots and a big black spot painted on the end of her nose. The baby was dressed in a kiddy dalmatian suit with a little black spot painted on his nose. Vera's marriage had hit a bump so that was the start of a reunion between Vera and me with a little Michael thrown in. That became a strenuous period for Vera. She had custody of her baby Michael every other week and severely missed him when he wasn't in her care. We made it through Christmas but she was remodeling her kitchen at her Cumberland house at the time, so that stress didn't help.

One evening, later that next year, Vera and the baby were at my house for dinner. Vera would schlep all of the baby stuff, crib and all, to my house, fix dinner, and then after a few minutes of play with me, the baby, and the cats, she would fall asleep in a chair, wake up later and schlep everything back to her house on Cumberland Road. We had occasional dinners out but that night she was at my house when the phone rang. It was one of Vera's cousins calling. I could tell that it was an alarming call and when Vera hung up the phone she said a cousin and family had been involved in a family tragedy. Vera had been close to her cousin. As children they liked art and would sit and draw together and as adults had been close. Vera and I attended the memorial service and I remember that day clearly, the emotional force of a memorial service plows a deep furrow in the heart and mind. On the way home Vera and I stopped for lunch. It was a tough time, what do you say at a time like that? Life sucks? Nice day? The sun is shining? Gee, I think I'll have a cheeseburger? Everything comes out sounding very stupid, even "I'm sorry." But the silence is even more painful.

To get away from it all, Vera and I took a trip with our friends Chuck and Stacey, to my condo on the island of Kauai. Vera tried very hard to have a good time but she was plagued by the mother "hard wiring" and she missed Michael. I would suppose she felt guilty about not being with Michael. On our flight back to L.A. we had some time to spend in Honolulu and decided to have a drink in Waikik at the Moana Surfrider Hotel. We sat under the giant banyon tree which shaded the patio and as we sat with our drinks in the shade of that big tree, enjoying the view of that white sand beach and beautiful Pacific, the talk turned to Vera's family and the concern everyone shared. The puzzlement of such a shattering event covered everyone's feelings with a haze of insecurity and depression. I couldn't imagine the pain and anguish Vera felt at the time. I was very little comfort for her. I just selfishly wanted to get on with what used to be our good life but events change lives, and you can't go back.

After our Hawaiian getaway we had a movie to finish drawing and eventually completed our work. The *Hercules* Los Angeles wrap party was memorable for being the largest and least enjoyable party to that date. I went alone but there were an estimated 5000 people there at the party to keep me company, that is, if I could just find a familiar face in a crowd of 5000 people on several different hotel floors. That party was also held in the Los Angeles Biltmore Hotel. There had been so many parties up to that time that my memories are smeared like a half-erased black board and sometimes it's hard to separate the smears of those memories into individual experiences.

Vera and I were still trying to manufacture a togetherness but the past events and present pressures made it difficult. In June the studio was flying us to New York to celebrate the opening of *Hercules* there and the departure date was a few days away. Vera decided that she didn't want to go so I went alone and by that I mean alone with two large passenger jets full of friends.

Some of my New York Hercules *birthday party friends*

The week in New York was splendid. We were again housed in the Regency Hotel on Park Avenue. That trip was useful for me because being surrounded by many friends in a place as busy as Manhattan leaves very little "feeling sorry for your self" time. I had Dan Lund and Michele as roommates and was never alone. By not directing my thoughts inward I had space in my head to save the outward experiences, which were many.

The one that fills my memory banks with multiplied confusion was the night we celebrated my birthday at Lucky Cheng's in New York's East Village. I was now officially older than most all of my friends and it was their idea to celebrate my birthday at Lucky Chengs. John Tucker and Dan Lund had come up with an idea which they knew would completely humiliate an old guy like me and would have the potential to stop my heart. We had all sat down at a long table and ordered drinks. My drink arrived just a few minutes before a great big, six foot two inch, adorable girl who happened to be black and a guy, came up to me and offered me a lap dance. John and Dan had conspired to destroy me that evening by buying a lap dance for me on my birthday but not with a cute sexy girl but a really big, attractive, sexy one of questionable gender named Tina. Dan and John knew the place was a classy Drag Queen Cabaret Dinner Theatre with a glut of jokes and props designed to send the least devout to confession. Actually the performers and waitresses were all very attractive "women" but Tina wasn't my type.

She straddled me, looking down, as she did her bumps and grinds.

My birthday surprise

I was thinking that I needed to get out of there or I needed to be very drunk and hadn't even finished my first drink. I stuck it out, bad pun, sorry, and much too every one's glee I was sufficiently embarrassed. The great big pretty girl finally finished her bit, which made me wonder how do they know when they're finished? I don't remember any music playing but I didn't want to give her bit any further thought. Everyone was fully delighted by my humiliating experience into the world of Tina and we proceeded to order dinner. The food was great and the sex-directed jokes were fun and everyone had a good time. I recovered from Tina's surprise assault on my senses and joined in the fun after I had rediscovered my more secure self. After dinner we all met in front of the restaurant and took pictures while waiting for cabs. To top my birthday evening off I left my reading glasses in the cab and spent the rest of the trip trying to read the small print which said, "Please remove all of your belongings from the cab."

We screened *Hercules* in the New Amsterdam Theater which is next to the Disney Store on 42nd Street in Times Square. That theater opened for the very first time on October 26, 1903. The PR at the time promised that the theater would "rival all other theaters" in the country. After years of a successful life the glamorous theater fell into disrepair. In 1993 The Walt Disney Company signed a ninety-nine-year lease for the building. The interior design incorporated extravagant use of the art nouveau style which The Walt Disney Company faithfully reproduced when restoring the building. It took several years and several million dollars to restore it to its original grandeur and it was beautiful. In April of 1997, the beautifully-restored theater opened with *Hercules* and I was there with my Disney friends. The street in front of the theater had bleachers set up and thousands of people were treated to a parade. After the outdoor ceremonies we entered the theater and saw a screening of our movie. I was honored to view our movie, *Hercules*, in that theater, a theater with its history. There is a beautiful book, *The New Amsterdam*, published by Hyperion Publishing which illustrates the history of the theater and The Walt Disney Company's restoration.

The later wrap party was spectacular. One evening buses carted us over to the World Trade Center for the party on the one-hundred and sixth floor of one of those really tall buildings. We were served Champagne while we waited for an elevator. John Tucker and I drank liberally to oil our nerves for a ride in an elevator the size of my living room which was going to take us up higher than all of the other buildings in New York. Neither John nor I are fond of being too far off the ground and the Champagne hardly helped. When we stepped out of the elevator the windows of the lobby were floor to ceiling so one could stand with your toes against the window and peer

Let the music play

straight down on the city of New York. It was thrilling. The party was in a very large room with a nice band and all of the food and drink one could consume. I have this framed photo of a fellow artist, Lieve Miesson, and myself, dancing at that party.

I look at that photo now and wonder, were those religious whacko terrorists, at that moment, in the planning stages of that horrendous 9/11/2001 Twin Towers event? That murderous act occurred about three and a half years after our marvelous party there. On February, 1993, four years before we had our party, the underground parking structure of the Twin Towers was blown up with a bomb exploded by a group allied to the same evil force. We were no doubt in the target when we had our party there. I keep that photo hanging in my hallway to remind me that life's moments are precious and far too few.

One of my thrills of the evening was having Jennifer Aniston sit on my lap. She was at the party with her boyfriend, Tate Donovan, who did the voice of Hercules in our film. I was sitting at a table when she happened by so I ask her if she would sit on my lap for a picture. She was very sweet, said yes, sat down and put her arm around my shoulder as my friend Michele was preparing for the photo opportunity. Jennifer and I struck a pose and Michele clicked her camera. Michele, with a look of disappointment and embarrassment, lowered her camera and announced that the camera was out of film.

There I sat with Jennifer on my lap trying to make small talk while Michele rustled up another camera. We got a picture; I thanked Jennifer, and I haven't heard from her since. Thanks to Michele I now have that picture hanging in my hall of fame.

During our free days Dan, Michele and I spent some time exploring Manhattan on foot. First

We make a lovely couple

the big Disney Store, of course, and then off to see the Flat Iron Building, then on to Wall Street, the big bronze bull, and a few museums and restaurants. It was a wonderful week but that fun had to end. We would go back to California and began the fun of contributing our art to another filmed story which will hopefully give millions of people a few hours of movie pleasure.

CHAPTER 21

Take Two Won't Do But Mulan Does

Flying back from New York the fun times were still bright in my memory. I arrived home to find Vera was no longer interested in a take two, a renewed twosome. Actually it was more like a two-and-a-half some because we did enjoy Michael's innocent company when she brought him along, but that was the end of that. The fun times were now clouded with thoughts of what to do about a big hole in my life, time to reinvent again. I did have my house on the hill that I enjoyed and I didn't have that depressing chore of finding some cheap, crusty, apartment to survive in, as I had experienced in the past. I got busy with work, *Mulan* was my next assignment. The project was headquartered in the Florida studio and we were the California annex. Barry Cook and Tony Bancroft were the directors. The visual effects supervisor in Florida was Dave Tidgwell and Joey Mildenberger was supervising the effects crew in California.

The picture was a difficult one because of many complicated effects scenes, lots of snow, water and the other environmental stuff. I think too that I might have been extra cranky due to the process of re-inventing myself, but rain, sleet, snow, hail, smoke and fire will not stop the visual effects animator from his work for that shall be his joy. But the joy was diminished a little for me because the cross-country Florida to California communication just didn't as work as well as face-to-face discussions. Even the technology of video communications wasn't as good as face time. But the picture was finished and turned out to be a very good looking movie and a good story. One of my favorite sequences to work on was the one with the giant paper dragon. The

167

dragon was occupied by the Hun's soldiers and was to appear threatening. Cobert Finnelly, an artist from Ireland, was helping me with some of the long shots but I was to animate the closer scenes as the dragon approached the steps and exploded as the bad guy Huns jumped out. The studio sent me to Florida to help out the crew there so I started working on the dragon scenes in Florida. I was filled with anxiety staring at that big white sheet of paper. I needed to draw a big Chinese paper dragon and have it come to life with my animation.

During my couple of weeks in Florida I had a room at The Boardwalk Hotel. It was a nice room with a coffee maker so I was happy in the morning to have coffee, first thing. A fun thing about working at the studio in Florida was that you were in Walt Disney World with the park, EPCOT, The World Showcase, the hotels and Pleasure Island just a short trip away. There were lots of restaurants and things to do and staying at the Boardwalk made my time off work seem like a vacation in Disney World. But Florida has those amazing storms which sometimes get in the way as I found out one evening when I left the studio and it began to rain. I borrowed an umbrella and as I walked out of the building the lightning started its scary dance in the sky. Just as I was going to dash to my car in the parking structure I noticed the umbrella I had borrowed was tipped with a metal pointy cap. I had a vision of a lightning strike hitting that little pointy cap so not to take chances with the lightning I folded up the umbrella and ran about seventy five yards to my rental auto in the pouring rain while the lightning was snapping and cracking all around me. Thinking about it later I realized I was no doubt safe in the rain because of Benjamin Franklin's curiosity. He invented the lightning rod and because of the Disney Company's severe attention to detail, all of the Disney buildings in Florida have an abundance of lightning rods, so they would have attracted the bolt which could have been meant for me.

I was pleased with those Chinese dragon scenes as they appear in the picture. I had accomplished my first drawings in Florida but later, back in California, I had trouble pleasing Barry Cook with the last close up scene of the dragon. The scene required that the Emperor's captain be standing in front of the dragon and the bad guys, Huns, who were concealed in the dragon would jump out to attack the captain and the Emperor. The Hun drawings weren't animated to make them explode out of the dragon but rather to jump out leisurely. During one of my sessions with Barry, via the video from Florida, Barry used the word explosive. That was it! Barry wanted an explosion of bad guys. The bad guys were holding me back, they weren't exploding out of the paper dragon and my dragon was dragin'. So I changed the animation timing of the Huns. I took out some of their drawings so they would explode from their hiding place in the dragon. At the next meeting with Barry he liked the scene and no one ever knew. But I do think he cut the scene a few frames too soon. A movie scene is like a sentence; if you leave off the last word or two of a sentence, spoken or written, or cut a frame or two too soon from a scene, it will appear to lack resolution.

At the completion of each movie the artists were all reviewed. The production managers and directors would grade the artists for their work and their ability as team members to work well with their fellow artists. When I received my review I was disturbed for Barry had given me a less than exemplary review for some of my more difficult moments. Being a cranky egotistical artist who had never received less than an excellent review I decided to write a few words on the back sheet of the review where it was stated "Remarks". Isn't that what it's for? I spewed out my thoughts of Barry's review under that word "Remarks" and sent it to HR, Human Resources. A few days later I received a phone call from the gentleman in charge of HR. The conversation which followed should have been conducted in the privacy of his room. Wonder why it wasn't? He opened the conversation after announcing himself by saying, "Dorse, do you really want to say this on your review?" To which I replied "Yes, that's why I wrote it on my review, under where it's stated, 'Remarks', I want those remarks to be read." He said he didn't think I should say that. After I exploded with a repeat of what I first said it became a yelling contest between to people who were no longer communicating. I never heard another word about my remarks and never knew what happened to that paperwork. For all I know the HR man in charge, as any good bureaucrat would do, just dropped the copy with my remarks in the wastebasket and replaced it with a copy of my review sans my remarks. The next time I saw Barry he didn't act as if he had read those remarks in which I had been critical of his directatorial duties.

The *Mulan* artists in L.A. were invited to a screening at the Director's Guild in Hollywood and we were bused over there one afternoon. As I walked into the very large lobby of the building there were many tables covered with Chinese food of every description. I saw Barry across the room, across the Chinese food. When our eyes met he scampered over and around the tables to say hi and to chat about the great movie we had finished. I was relieved for he presented nothing but warmth without a trace of animosity. Later we decided to have a lunch together. Barry and I, we were okay.

The California crew screening of *Mulan* occurred at the Hollywood Bowl, an outdoor venue. The wrap party was held at the famous Hollywood Palladium. My first visit to the Palladium was in 1953. I was a senior student at Burbank High School and had a date with Elva Fisher, a sophomore. That evening we went to the Hollywood Palladium and danced to the Harry James

Orchestra. Now that is a special memory. I think I had more fun that night with Elva than I did at the *Mulan* wrap party.

Mulan opened June 19, 1998, to good reviews. Its first weekend gross was just over $22 million and went on to earn a reported total of over three-hundred million dollars world wide, so the artists did good.

CHAPTER 22

A Hawaiian Bonus to the Jungles of Tarzan

After finishing *Mulan* I took a trip to Hawaii to collect my personal stuff from my condo on Kauai. The condo sale was final so I had all of my wall art packaged for shipment and took a lot of stuff to the local Salvation Army. I packed Vera's tropical hats, her teeny weeny bikinis, lava-lavas and memories, in my luggage, to give them to her when I returned home. I thought this was a good time to sell the condo for the old guys on the board of directors were all wealthy, honest, upright fun guys and their management skills were superb. That was a plus for the buyer. I actually miss the old guys and their Mai Tai's. This wasn't the best period of my life but it was fun when I visited the island for the annual owners' meetings and our annual owners' party at the pool. The old guys treated me special and their wives' attention would do wonders for my ego; I think they thought I had the Disney artist mojo

Those guys got us through all of the work that had to be done on the exteriors of the buildings after Hurricane Iniki did its best to force the island back into the Stone Age. There were seventy condos on ten tropically-landscaped acres there, fronting the Pacific Ocean. Repairing the hurricane damage was an enormous and expensive task and the interaction with the insurance companies was ongoing for years, but our old guys came through. Once all of the work was done the place looked better than ever. But the large trees in the forests had to be waited on for there was much damage to them. Fortunately the tropical islands are very good for plants and in a few years the forests were all looking new again.

I loved my Jaguar XK8

That trip to Hawaii wasn't all pleasant though, for I had to say goodbye to the condo and many good memories but I was going back California to good news from my negotiating agent at the studio. While in Hawaii I received a phone call from her, she was offering me a signing bonus that I would receive when I came back to Burbank and signed a new contract. I actually talked her into more money than she had offered so when I a got back to California I bought a Jaguar XK8 convertible, anthracite black with a tan interior.

A guy had bought it for himself as a birthday present and decided he liked his Toyota SUV better. It was a one-owner car with only ten thousand miles on it so I saved a bundle. Silly life, it knocks you down and then gives you another opportunity to claw your way back up.

I had an evening flight back to L.A. which was going to depart at ten o'clock. I always try to be early for everything and I arrived at the airport early that night. I had an interesting book which I was part way through so I sat down in the lobby to read until boarding time. As I sat there a group of people entered the lobby in a boisterous party spirit and were taking pictures and attending to an attractive blond in the group. I was happy for them but feeling alone and out of contact with a party spirit. When it was time to board I got in line with those entering the aircraft and as I boarded, I noticed the party people were still saying their goodbyes. The aircraft wasn't packed and I found a window seat, I like window seats. I waited for someone to fill the two seats beside me hoping that the seats would remain empty so I might be able to lay down for a nap. As other people boarded the aircraft and began that annoying process of storing their carry on bags, the blond that was in the goodbye group arrived at my row and promptly claimed the aisle seat which left an empty seat between us. After she got settled, to break the ice, I extended my hand which held a small box of cookies and said "Would you like a cookie?" It wasn't the greatest opening line to start with a complete stranger but I hadn't had dinner and the cookies were all I had to eat. I thought she might be hungry too. Well it did start the conversation so she told me about the group she was with. She had been working as a nurse in a hospital out in Waimea, Kauai and the group was her friends and fellow workers. She was headed for Spokane, Washington to work at a hospital there. She didn't tell me what hospital, only Spokane. It was a red eye flight so each of us eventually fell asleep and awoke the next morning as we landed in Los Angeles. She had to catch a connecting flight so we said our nice to meet you stuff and the last I saw of her she was checking out the flight display. I thought she was cute but regretfully didn't think I would ever see her again. I didn't even remember her name.

Back home I was fortunate to have a good, fun job. I was beginning work on *Tarzan,* which was a big picture with lots of effects, but I kept thinking it might be fun to see if I could track down that attractive Swedish blond. Always when working, those little flash frames of memory appear in your mind when the brain relaxes for a moment. My flash frames were of her. Eventually I found time at home to get on the phone and call hospitals in Washington that were located around the city of Spokane. I would get someone in their HR unit and would ask if a nurse just started work there, a nurse who had just flown in from Hawaii. About the third hospital the lady said yes, that would be Kristin. I ask if I could speak to her and she said no, but offered to pass my number along. So I received a call and that began a relationship that lasted three years.

Kristin, I didn't know her name, but I played detective and found her

At first we did an abundance of telephone dancing which led to me to think that she might be a potential co-pilot to help me steer my life, someone to share life with and give me more to live for than just my hedonistic existence. She actually had a photo of me, taken before we had met, sitting in the background reading my book in the airport lobby when she was having her goodbye party as we were preparing to fly out of Kauai. I wanted to get to know her better so I had her fly down to Los Angeles a few times when we both had a few days to spend together. My friend, Don Klein, has a favorite quote: "Desperate people do desperate things." Looking back I do think I was tired of living alone and was caught up in the excitement of tracking down the prey and no doubt fueled by desperation. And detective work is fun. It wasn't an easy sell but I convinced her that we could try living together and if it didn't work out we could, as grown ups, just mutually decide to dissolve the relationship. Now, is that foolish or what? She quit her job in Spokane, came to Glendale, and we started a domestic gathering. She found work at the Glendale Memorial Hospital in the Oncology Department. That was tough for her. She was too caring and sensitive for that environment. People who work in the oncology departments of hospitals have to deal with people dying on a daily basis and it has to be tough.

Our relationship had started off as they all do but after about a year of living together the relationship started to dissolve in a blur of misunderstandings and painful silliness. I learned that I was kind of protective of my space and that doesn't work when two people are trying to live in a sharing mode. It was tough for her because it was my house, my space, my identity, and she was trying to fit into it. We finally did agree that it would be better if we split up. She decided to move back to Minnesota, her home, and try to settle there. The day she left was difficult for the both of us. We hugged and tried to comfort each other as best we could but it was painful. Away she went, reluctantly, and that was that. I still hear from her once in awhile and I'm happy that she's happy now.

Tarzan was a fun picture to work on. A herd of elephants traipsing around in water is fun, and for us special effects artists there was lots of water; rivers, waterfalls and lots of splashing elephants. But conflict, which makes a good story, was absent from my experience when working on *Tarzan*, I was just having fun working. The conflict in my life, at this time, was in my domestic setting but I could escape into my fun work and hide from the domestic problem that would eventually need to be faced and painfully solved and finally was.

The studio was hiring more people with a Master of Business Administration, MBA, into our animation setting. I wasn't privy to the behind the scenes happenings for I was sheltered in my visual effects groove. I have found that everyone lives in their particular groove or channel and their knowledge and experience doesn't overlap too far into differing people's grooves. My doctor, trained in Western medicine, doesn't have a furrow that overlaps much with mine. He can be reluctant to hear me out about proven alternative medical solutions which may conflict with western medical studies. He is especially reluctant if I've discovered this info on the internet. He sees me as an artist and doesn't want me trying to slip into his groove and of course I wouldn't expect him to be able to do my job.

The studio's success with our animated films was waning and, apparently, management felt that a solution might be with someone in a new groove, one outside of the artist's groove. Someone that knew more about business and making money than about creating art that sells. When selling creative works, that is paintings, animated films, live action movies, anything that is the final result of an artists efforts, everyone and every thing else aside from the artist is part of the support group, there to support the artist. In the case of the studio and the MBA's, the artist became part of the support group for the MBA's. An artist can benefit by that training to take care of the business side of selling art but the art should come first. The studio's MBA's, the support group, were telling the artists how to do their art and of course the success expected was not forthcoming because the proverbial cart was before the horse. With all of this said I'm not sure we can put all of the blame for the decline of our success on management. To make an animated film or any film requires the mutual effort of many artists working together. Artists by their very nature tend to be more solitary than group-oriented. To have several hundred artists come together and accomplish a successful work of art as complicated as a film, animated or otherwise, is a rare phenomenon indeed. Of the hundreds of films made every year, the majority fall by the wayside, never noticed by the greater world and never to win their place in history as a work of art. *Tarzan* wasn't one of those. *Tarzan* had more artist input and less management control. It was a successful film.

Tarzan did well at the box office with a reported world-wide gross to date of $448 million. It will live in the Disney library of successful films forever. I'm happy my name is listed in the credits along with hundreds of other artists that worked very hard to make it a success. I'm sure we had a fun wrap party for *Tarzan* but I just can't find a ghost of it in my memory. Must have been that my personal life was a blotter of my existence, a sturdy paper towel wipe of my past.

CHAPTER 23

IN The Groove With Computers on the Move

After finishing *Tarzan* I was assigned to *The Emperor's New Groove*. Yes, I still had a job. *The Emperor's New Groove* started life as an animated film called *Kingdom of the Sun*, a large story by Roger Allers and Matthew Jacobs to be produced by Randy Fulmer. But there were some problems with the screenplay: the story development was taking to long. There was much pulling and pushing in an effort to get a good story which could be turned into an animated film in time for the release date. Management decided to shoot for a simpler story but kept the setting which was the country of Peru in South America. Mark Dindal was to direct and Randy Fulmer was producing. It wasn't *Kingdom of the Sun* any more, it was *The Emperor's New Groove*. Both Mark and Randy were former special effects artists and both endowed with an edgy sense of humor. I had worked with both guys on many movies so I knew it would be fun. We had what might be called rapport. Not sure what Mark and Randy would call it but I'll stick with rapport. There is a documentary film, produced by Trudie Styler, called *The Sweatbox* which documents the pain and anguish of the maneuvering to get *The Kingdom of the Sun/The Emperor's New Groove* made into a movie. Trudie Styler is the wife of Sting. Sting composed the song, *My Funny Friend and Me* along with David Hartley. Sting performed it for the movie and the song was nominated for an Academy Award for Best Original Song.

While the development people were struggling to get the story of *The Emperor's New Groove* to a point where the rest of us could start work on it, Roy Disney was pushing to get *Fantasia/2000* completed; It was an updated version of the original *Fantasia* with a few new sequences. While Mark and Randy, with their story people, were squashing and stretching the story for *The Emperor's New Groove* into a screenplay, I was put to work on *Fantasia/2000*, The *Rhapsody in Blue* segment, one of my favorite pieces of music. I worked with Eric Goldberg, one of the several directors on the picture. Eric is a talented animator with many credits including the animation of Genie in *Aladdin*. He was an easy director to work with. He would tell me what he wanted and all I had to do was do it the way I thought he wanted it. The scenes were complicated, fun, and took some effort to accomplish.

I took a break from work and went to a barbeque one night, out in the hills of Woodland Hills. My chiropractor, Dr. Singh, was throwing a party for a few friends and neighbors. His next door neighbor happened to be Joe Alves. I first met Joe in 1956 when I was hired by Walt Disney Productions to work in the special effects animation department and Joe was an assistant animator. My memory is a bit hazy but I think Joe left the studio about the time we started work on *Sleeping Beauty*. I lost track of Joe after I was drafted into the Army but I would occasionally hear his name mentioned during my meanderings. Joe's artistic talent and motivation along with his ability to avoid those flyin' chunks allowed him to arrive on the doorstep of a certain Mr. Spielberg. Steven Spielberg was preparing to make what would become a big box office smash. Joe's timing and talent were such that he became an art director for Steven Spielberg. He worked as an art director on many films but I think his proudest moment had to be as the production designer on one of the biggest movie hits on record up to that time, a movie called *Jaws*. When Joe and I got together that night at Dr. Singh's, Joe said something to me that peaked my proudness. During our rambling conversation about our past experiences, of the films we had worked on, and our personal lives, he concluded by saying, "Dorse, we touched greatness." I was flattered that he included me in that statement.

At the Disney studio, for the people who liked to draw animation, a storm was brewing on our horizon. The commercial success of CG films, computer generated films, from other studios were becoming a serious threat to those of us who like to draw our movies, referred to as 2d films. The people who spend their millions of dollars to make a movie want to make one that will return a profit and that's what the CG films were doing. The audiences enjoyed the new look of the CG films and money, like water or electricity, follows the path of least resistance. Our 2d artists were getting nervous as the studio brought in more computer people.

The studio always had a few pots cooking on the stove and at that time one pot had a film being developed called *Wild Life*. It was to be a more stylized art design and animated in CG, a story about Manhattan night life which Roy Disney later shelved. Another pot had a more promising idea cooking called *Chicken Little* but it was another CG project so things were looking gloomy for those of us who like to draw animation. But the project which would be ready for the 2d artists after *The Emperor's New Groove* was to be called *Home on the Range*.

After finishing my work on *Fantasia/2000,* I went to work on *The Emperor's New Groove*. It was a fun, light hearted, romp of a movie to work on and we had no calamities along the way. At least, there were no calamities that I was involved in but the big guys had a tiff. The unfortunate death of Disney's President, Frank Wells, in 1994, left a vacuum which created a power struggle. There was a political scuffle between Jeffrey Katzenberg, the man in charge of motion picture production at the studio, and CEO Michael Eisner. The end result of that flurry was that Katzenberg quit the studio and co-founded Dreamworks SKG with Steven Spielberg and David Geffen. On March 31, 2000, Dreamworks SKG released *The Road to El Dorado*, a 2d hand drawn film, which was set in South America. *The Emperor's New Groove*, released December 15, 2000, was moderately successful. It was reported to have grossed more than $89 million domestic and the total for world wide release was over $169 million. *The Road toEl Dorado* had a domestic gross of close to $60 million. Don't know how they figure all of that out, but it was good.

And yes, I remember *The Emperor's New Groove* wrap party. It was held in Los Angeles in a building that was built for the Elks club in the 1920's. It is now The Park Plaza hotel which has maintained the beautiful original art deco style. The neighborhood is a bit shaky for it is directly across the street from the infamous MacArthur Park of Los Angeles. I had my Jag XK8 sports car and my blond Swedish girlfriend, both icons of symbolic success. Both were very attractive, but for different reasons of course, and either one would be attractive to the unscrupulous types that inhabited that neighborhood. I had possibly put myself in the position of risking my life to save my Jag or my girlfriend, or both. Fortunately the evening went smoothly except for the band that played so loud that dancing in that room was deafeningly difficult and talking was totally out of the question. But we had another large room with gambling, pretend of course, and lots of food and drink so it was a proper celebration for the completion of another film. After the party my girlfriend and I guardedly scurried to my car and fled back to the safety of my home in the hills of Glendale. Another party, another night, the world was good.

CHAPTER 24

Home on the Range
Then out to Pasture

After *The Emperor's New Groove* our next project was a movie called *Home on the Range*. It was to be a 2d film with computer animated props. That was another troubled production in that it started out as a story about a cow in the old west that had to deal with civilization moving westward and how that migration changed life there. After much troubling story development, someone, I don't know who, finally decided that the story didn't work. We needed to start over. It finally ended up as a story about a country woman who was going to lose her farm if she couldn't raise the money for the mortgage. The result would be that her beloved animals would be sent away to be homeless. She decided that her three cows could capture a cattle rustler and she could collect the reward and have the money to save her farm and the animals. Some sort of a story about the westward migration worked for Dreamworks SKG in 2002. They released a movie with a more serious story called *Spirit: Stallion of the Cimarron,* co-directed by Lorna Cook, a friend of mine and Kelly Asbury. That story was about a stallion in the west that clashed with forces that had the potential to curtail the freedom of any horse. But the stallion won and heroically established his western independence.

The Disney animation studio now was inhabited by an abundance of very bright computer people and for *Home on the Range* we were going to use computers to animate props, mine cars and trains. I even did some of that myself. In fact I was kind of proud of the work I did. In a scene that had the train engine roaring down the tracks, away from the camera, I animated the big steam locomotive using the computer. The computer model had been well built and there were a lot of moving parts so I took advantage of that to make it look like a seriously-speeding, rattling, steam locomotive engine. I also used the computer to animate some of the mine cars and that was fun but it was the beginning of the end for my 47 year drawing career.

One day my granddaughter Holly and I were discussing the films I had worked on. I think she was twelve or thirteen years old at the time. *The Lion King* was the top of the ladder of our success and after that film our movies were gradually becoming less capable of attracting the necessary audiences. Holly said, "Grandpa, just tell them to make more films with furry talking animals." But there was something more serious looming and it wasn't furry talking animals, it was toys! The year after *The Lion King* was released an animation company called Pixar, with an ex-Disney computer animation pioneer named John Lasseter at the helm, released a little movie with the title of *Toy Story*. It was the first animated feature film constructed entirely on computers and it was a big hit. The pressure was on for the Disney animators to get into the 3d business. This meant that we 2d artists, drawing types, would not be useful to the company unless we suddenly acquired the necessary computer skills. And to make matters worse, the last several 2d films which Disney's studio released didn't live up to our earlier successes.

Marlon West, a talented artist and visual effects animator was the supervisor of special effects on *Home on the Range,* but we had a digital effects lead animator, Michael Kaschalk, to approve the 3d work before submitting it to Marlon for his final effects approval. The computer and 3d animation was

Marlon West

creeping, no, more like roaring into our abode.

Home on the Range was not one of our proudest moments. There were even some artists who didn't want their names on the credits. I didn't mind, I liked my steam locomotive. The movie is reported to have a world wide box office gross of over $70 million but it was said to have cost more than that to make. Our crew screening was held at Universal City Walk and the wrap party was at a large western-themed restaurant and bar there. The party was much fun but all very scaled down compared to the past parties.

It was March of the next year, 2002; the studio in Burbank announced that it was going to layoff several hundred artists. It was later announced that the Florida studio as well as the one in Paris were closing, which would mean another three hundred employees out of work. Most of my artist friends were out of work, laid-off by Walt Disney Feature Animation. For them it would be no more going to work in the building with the big blue sorcerers' apprentice hat, the hat which can be seen from the Ventura Freeway as you're passing by. But I was fortunate in that the studio was going to maintain my employment for they felt with my experience in effects animation I could be trained to use the computer to do the work. Dan Lund, moved by the disastrous events, wrote and directed a documentary with the title, *Dream on Silly Dreamer,* which covers this period of the rise and fall of Walt Disney Feature Animation and the artists who experienced it. It was produced by Tony West with a little help from Roy Disney. Dan and Tony are movie maker friends of mine; they're master effects animators who were fortunate enough to have worked and lived the dream with us, while it lasted.

So the studio laid off my friends, took away my pencil and paper and gave me a computer to use for animating effects. Oh yes, and another thing. One day a gentleman came to my room with my big window and said, "We are going to move company lawyers into this nice little wing of which your room is a part of so you're going to have to vacate this room with the nice big window."

So the MBA's had taken over the story department, the computer guys had taken over the animation, and some company lawyers were taking over my room with the nice big window. Humm, this meant I would have to move

My big window

L to R, Dan Lund, John Tucker, me and Tony West.
All serious at the Dream On Silly Dreamer mix

back to the room which I had occupied when working on *The Hunchback of Notre Dame*, a room without a big window or any window. My art school buddy, Bob Elder, used to say, "A step backward might be a step in the right direction" but this wasn't what I called a "right" direction. I found it disturbing and it caused a germ in my think tank to start sprouting.

I began the job packing my stuff in boxes, videos, mementos and coffee mugs to cart it all to the inside windowless room. So began my days of going downstairs in the morning to study effects animation on the computer for an hour and then coming back to my room to spend a few frustrating minutes trying to find a place for my stuff and then sitting down to the computer. The computer would then show me how basically stupid I was by not responding to what I thought were the proper buttons to push to achieve glorious effects animation, so it was garbage in, garbage out. I couldn't make it do the stuff the instructor had drilled into me downstairs so the rest of the day was boring, frustrating, and sometimes alarming. A germ in my brain's think tank started to grow and it looked like it had a blossom sprouting. Yes, the blossom was looking just like a white flag of surrender.

One morning I came back to my windowless, cell like room and was emptying the last of my boxes when it occurred to me that I really didn't have to work, I didn't need to surrender to their needs, I could capture my own moment. It was a realization which I think had been in my subconscious, but which I denied up to that point when it washed over me like a fresh shower. The lid came off my id, my instinctual needs erupted all over my ego, and my conscious self let go of the need to have my identity identified with my work. What to do now? I would have a pension and social security, which I had been collecting since I turned sixty-five, and some investments. I had been paid to draw effects, to doodle for dollars, for forty-seven years, and now I was going to be paid for not drawing. I would probably still be at the studio drawing to this day if we were still animating 2d films but at that time the studio had decided not to. I bravely faced my moment and decided, yes, I could live on less, without a weekly paycheck! Yes, I'm going to retire!

So I went to the man in charge of Human Resources; I don't remember his name, he hadn't been there long. I told him that I wanted out of my contract, I wanted to retire. He said, "Well, Dorse, we will have to have a meeting, I'll get back to you." Oh, those meetings. A week or so later he got back to me and it was all good. I had eight weeks paid vacation coming to me and he said that I could stop working at the end of October. They would rescind my contract and pay me for November and December. That would give me time to contact the pension fund and have that set up to start January 1. Wow, I'm gonna do it.

One glitch occurred in my retirement process. The man in charge of HR quit and went to work for The Gap. He left his assistant in control and as a result I didn't have the customary retirement party or the goodbye pluses. Or maybe no one noticed that I had retired. I had my picture taken for the company paper, *Disney Newsreel*, and it was published with a small quote by me, "My career has been an amazing adventure, filled with many wonderful people in many wonderful places, now I'm going to rest." But actually that wasn't totally accurate. I wrote "My career has been an amazing adventure in many wonderful places, with many wonderful people and some not so wonderful, now I'm going to rest." Well, everybody can't be wonderful, but my statement was edited for obvious reasons. On that last working day, October first, 2003, I walked out of the studio, found my Jag in the parking structure and drove home. It was a lonely drive home and that was that.

A couple of months after I retired, a big box was delivered to my door,
and to my surprise it contained this 11 by 13 inch, walnut and stainless steel,
Thank You note from Mickey Mouse.

CHAPTER 25

Making Room for the New Guys

OK, retirement joke. I wake up in the morning with nothing to do and by the time I go to bed I'm only half finished. The author of that joke is unknown to me but obviously they were successfully retired. That has also been my retired experience. Working people ask me what I do with my time and I tell them that I do what they do on their break at work but I get to do that all day. I don't know how I worked all of those years and took care of business. I never thought I was that good. I bought stuff, sold stuff, owned rental houses, homes, cars and condos. Refinanced, made loans, and paid loans. Hired and fired; gardeners, housekeepers, investment advisors and stock brokers. Pleasing wives and girlfriends, forced divorces, new starts and broken hearts. Traveled here and there, got laid-off and paid-off, new jobs and new bosses. Tax shelters with problems and IRS frights and sleepless nights. Tax extensions and reinvention, all the while taking care of the everyday things required for life and working long hours too. But it was mostly good.

Each morning I wake up, roll over to the side of the bed and sit up. As I lower my feet to the floor I rejoice with the feeling that gravity is still working and that it pushes my feet to the floor, or pulls my feet to the floor, depending on which scientist's theory you except. Whatever the force, it allows me to be vertical again after a restful sleep. I turn on the TV to make sure that some bozo hasn't blown the world to bits. I see the freeways jammed with all of those ambitious people who are lucky enough to have a job or better yet, a career. I don't miss the morning traffic. Even though living in Glendale is just a short drive to the Walt Disney studio, the traffic is always bad in the morning. I feel blessed and am very happy that all of those people sitting on the freeways are hard-working, responsible people going to work every day to pay my social security. I appreciate their efforts. They're out there early in the morning, concerned about their work, their careers, their families, eager to do a good days work and contribute their energy to our good life.

I do feel blessed. At the beginning of my retirement it was lonely for I missed the hubbub of work. The people, the drawing, animating special effects, all of the interaction with fellow artists when figuring out how to make animation stuff work for a movie and I missed all of my friends. I came home to the only breathing creatures there, my cats, Maryann and Ginger, and they had a very limited vocabulary. I soon realized that a person who has to have their day structured, their time organized, will suffer in retirement unless they have many interests which propel them through their day. I've found that to be retired or rich enough that one never has to work requires that one be capable of living with unstructured time, that is living with time not structured by outside forces such as a job. To be retired one has to structure one's own time and that requires an interest in and curiosity about living life.

Many people in our past who discovered useful facts about living life and the world about us were people who were secure enough in their worldly goods to have the time, the passion, and the curiosity to explore, study and

Maryann wants to edit

share their discoveries with the world. People whose lives have been their work and have few interests outside of that work will have to keep working for they will not live long in retirement without other interests. I realized some time ago that to be bored is to be boring and the cure for boredom is an interest in living, a passion. Of course it is okay for people to continue working if their work provides them with an interest in the life they want. I do think that I would probably still be working if the studio would have continued a 2d film schedule. But then again, if I was still employed I would never get to that stack of books I'm trying to read or get around to finishing this memoir.

After I had adjusted to the aloneness of retirement, I did have a bit of a problem dealing with a day that was totally mine. At first it seemed so self serving not to be doing something important, like earning a living. I think I felt guilty for not going to work, just doing stuff that I wanted to do for no one but myself. I do things for others now but I do it because I enjoy it. I have setup financial portfolios for my brother, for friends, and have done some Photoshop work for others. But actually this, in the popular sense of the word, is selfish of me because I do it for my own pleasure and it just happens to benefit someone else. But the popular definition of selfish seems incorrect. In the big picture a person must put self first in order to be strong and capable when called on to take care of those you love or are responsible for. Okay, I feel better now.

After I retired it took a year or so before I could just sit and read without feeling like I needed to be doing something important. But the wonderful thing about retirement is that I can do all of the things that interest me whenever I want to.

My health is important to me so I go to the gym mostly every other day and try to work out for a therapist's hour, that is at least 50 minutes. I can stop writing and take a nap now or go discover a few new sounds on my guitar, or go to an art museum. But I won't because I'm having fun writing this in the hope that you're now having fun reading it.

I still get to attend studio functions. On Sunday, January 10, 2010, I attended a celebration of Roy E. Disney's life. There was a brunch for one thousand Disney people in the Grand Ballroom of the Hollywood Highland Center, home of the Kodak theater. A brunch for one thousand people is a lot of brunching. After the brunch there was a three hour presentation across the street at the El Capitan Theater, which the Disney Company owns. The service was produced and hosted by Don Hahn and was a splendid memorial to Roy. That day, January 10, would have been Roy's eightieth birthday. He died on December 16, 2009. I remember talking cars with him a few times. He liked cars and chatted with me as if

I had the money to buy a Ferrari. I had my Jag then and he had a Ferrari, and probably several other cars. He was telling me his Ferrari spent a lot of time in the shop for it was high strung. Another time he told me about losing one of his other Ferraris in a parking garage. It was a dark purple kind of color but in the parking garage it looked black. He wasn't looking for a black Ferrari so it took him some time to realize there just weren't a lot of Ferrari's of his model in the parking garage. In fact, only one and it was his dark purple one.

I talked to him at a party which was held to honor him for his fifty years at the studio. That was after the studios had decided that computer generated animated films was their next ticket to success. I suggested to him that if the studio would do a hand-drawn 2d film they could hire the artists at union scale. It would be less expensive than *The Lion King* days. He seemed to like the idea. In October, 2009, I wrote him a letter wishing him well for I had heard that he was sick. I had just reread the book *Storming the Magic Kingdom* and I wanted to thank him again for saving The Walt Disney Company. I received a shaky, hand-written response from him in November and he thanked me for my "kind words" and said "It's great to hear from you". He said if I got a chance I should "see Waking Sleeping Beauty, it will sure bring back some memories, all the best for many more years to come. Roy." He wrote that a month before he left us.

Earlier I did see *Waking Sleeping Beauty* when Don Hahn screened it for us at the studio and it did bring back a lot of good memories. I feel honored that I am still part of The Walt Disney Company. I occasionally go over to the studio and have lunch with my friends who still work there. As a retiree from the company I have my life time Silver Pass which allows me to enter any of the Disney parks with a few friends or family. I still feel privileged and enjoy walking around the Walt Disney studio lot thinking of those days in the 50's when I first worked there as a young man.

I didn't know that Roy's illness was terminal when I wrote him that letter. I heard of his death on December 16, one month after he wrote to me. He was the protector and steward of Disney animation. His saving The Walt Disney Company allowed me to return there to work on *Who Framed Roger Rabbit* and to continue my career through all of the wonderful animated films we did after that. I framed my letter along with his note and it's displayed in my house.

At the memorial celebration, Robert Iger, the president and CEO of The Walt Disney Company presented a picture on the theater screen of the animation building with new large letters, across the entrance, spelling out "Roy E. Disney Animation Building".

Mr. Iger surprised us by proposing that the animation building be re-named for Roy

The Burbank cancer center, Roy spent his money on other things besides Ferraris

Now my mornings begin with my ambling to the kitchen with my cat Maryann walking beside me; we lost Ginger to an illness last year. Maryann stays at my side for she wants to make sure I'm going to continue to the kitchen to feed her for she knows that sometimes I get distracted and head off in a different direction. After I set her breakfast dish of fish down, I make coffee. I like my coffee first thing but only after I feed Maryann. I check the financial news and have breakfast. Then on to the computer to check the day's emails and answer those that need it and forward those that need that. Then I continue my work, writing my next book. It's going to be about the women in my life.

The Head, the Hearts, and Other Parts
An Expose of Dorse's Underside

Chapter 1
Mother

In the beginning there was the word, and the word was Mom.

Afterword

One day it occurred to me that my professional career has cross-dissolved into my grand daughter's life. I realized that she is a continuance of my life and as such she is driven by her art. The beginning of her artist life is an appropriate ending for the story of my career as an artist.

Years ago, long before my grand daughter's beginning, a neighborhood child came over to visit. During our chat she said she was bored and my response was rather off the top of my head, I replied, "You're not bored, you're boring." I said "You don't seem interested in anything, no curiosity, nothing to talk about, to think about, and this makes you feel bored." She was very cute, with her head nodding approval; she seemed to understand what I meant. So a little girl made me aware that when I thought I was bored it was because I was boring, not interested or interesting. "Who wants a boring person for company?"

And now my grand daughter Holly is never bored. She has fun using her head to direct the passions of her heart. Holly is driven by her desire to create art in the form of sculptures, costumes, creature designs, drawings and music composition. Her interest in writing and the Harry Potter series inspired her to get a degree in Medieval Studies. She is a very good writer and writes very clever copy for the products she designs, constructs, and sells on her Internet store.

She is employed in the animatronics field helping to fabricate the creatures one sees at Disneyland, and other parks and museums. She has won costume design contests and received awards for her efforts. A few months ago Holly rounded up a few friends to help her design and build costumes for the skit they performed at the costume contest at the 2010 San Diego California Comic Con Convention in July, winning the Judges Award.

Holly was very excited to have been chosen to appear in the Comic Con feature-length theatrical documentary, *Comic Con Episode Four: A Fan's Hope*, directed by Morgan Spurlock and produced by Stan Lee, Joss Whedon and Harry Knowles. The film follows several Comic Con fans up to their participation at the convention. Holly and her troop was filmed during the construction of their costumes and Holly' sculpting the head for "Grunt", a main creature of the skit which is a sequence from the video game, Mass Effect II.

As an artist, her passion fills her days and I have no doubt that she will have a life, not devoid of struggle, but one which will bring her much joy. The Force persists, ever onward.

About the Author

Dorse worked as an artist for 48 years, more than half of those years for Walt Disney Feature Animation as an effects animator. His work can be seen in most of the Disney animated films from *Sleeping Beauty,* through *Beauty and the Beast, The Lion King,* and his last film before retirement, *Home on the Range.* As an artist, he animated special effects such as; storms, water, fire, shadows, explosions, etc., all of which created the environment for the cartoon characters that inhabit the films.

Dorse lives in Glendale, California, on the southern point of the Verdugo Mountains, just a few miles from Walt Disney Studios. He enjoys the company of his strictly indoor cat, Maryann, and takes pleasure in his hill-side view of downtown Los Angeles. Dorse experiences an occasional rattle snake, visiting deer, apprehensive coyote, and many lizards around his neighborhood so he's very careful to make sure Maryann never ventures out into the wild.

He continues to be creative with his writing and his art as he tries to find time to read the numerous books and magazines which cover his interests in art, science, people, music, politics and history. Dorse still enjoys his relationships with the animation special effects artists he has mentored over the years and continues to associate with many of the people in the business of making animated movies.

My Crazy Books

The following is a list of the more important books which helped me to find my road less traveled. The titles are not in any order of importance for all knowledge is equally important in the search for wisdom.

Man's Search for Meaning ... Viktor E. Frankl

The Prophet ... Kahlil Gibran

The Mad Man ... Kahlil Gibran

Psycho-Cybernetics ... Maxwell Maltz, M.D.

The Road Less Traveled ...M. Scott Peck, M.D.

Games People Play ... Eric Berne, M.D.

Transactional Analysis... Eric Berne, M.D.

Speak For Yourself ... Jessica Somers Driver

The Way of Zen ... Alan W. Watts

This Is It ... Alan W. Watts

The Wisdom of Insecurity ... Alan W. Watts

How I found Freedom In an Unfree World ... Harry Browne

I'm OK You're OK ... Thomas A. Harris, M.D.

Passages ... Gail Sheehy

On Becoming a Person ... Carl R. Rogers

Gestalt Therapy ... Frederic Perls, Ralph F. Hefferline, PaulGoodman

Professional Summary

Schooling

The Art Center College of Design in Los Angeles, California, majoring in automobile and product design.

Work Experience

I worked as a sculptor, and designer, on the 1958 Mark IV Lincoln Continental at the Design Center of The Ford Motor Company, Detroit, Michigan. Was artist, designer, animator, on military technical films for Technical Communications Inc., Santa Monica, California. Worked for the Lytle Corporation, Culver City, California, as illustrator, animator. Designed, animated and directed educational films for Film Designers, a division of Educational Materials Corporation, out of St. Paul Minnesota. Was a partner in Image Arts, a California Partnership, producing educational and technical films for the Navy and various clients. Designed, supervised and animated feature film special effects for Don Bluth Productions aka Sullivan Bluth Productions. Twenty years as special effects designer, animator, and supervisor, for Walt Disney Feature Animation, Burbank, California.

Motion Picture Film Credits

2001 *Home on the Range*

2000 *The Emperors New Groove*

1999 *Tarzan*

1999 *Fantasia/2000*

1998 *Mulan*

1997 *Hercules*

1996 *The Hunch Back of Notre Dame*

1995 *Pocahontas*

1994 *The Lion King*

1992 *Aladdin*

1991 *Beauty and the Beast*

1989 *The Little Mermaid*

1988 *Oliver and Company*

1988 *Who Framed Roger Rabbit*

1988 *The Land Before Time*

1986 *An American Tail*

1982 *The Secret of NIHM*

1980 *Xanadu*

1979 *The Black Hole*

1977 *Pete's Dragon*

1977 *The Rescuers*

1961 *One Hundred and One Dalmatians*

1956 *Sleeping Beauty*

Featurett/TV/Video Credits

1993 *Trail Mix Up*

1990 *Roller Coaster Rabbit*

1990 *The Prince and the Pauper*

1984 *Space Ace* (video game)

1983 *Dragon's Lair* (video game)

1980 *Banjo the Woodpile Cat*

1978 *The Small One*

1974 *The City That Forgot Christmas* (TV)

1971 *Easter Is* (TV)

1970 *Christmas Is* (TV)

Affiliations

Academy of Motion Picture Arts and Sciences

The Animation Guild Local 839 (TAG)

The Creative Talent Network